WOMEN & WEED

CENTENNIAL BOOKS

CONTENTS

5

A
Cannabis
Primer

A cannabis plant contains about 60 cannabinoids.

WEED WORDS

A guide to some of the marijuana
world's most important terminology.

For anyone who is just now discovering cannabis, either medical or recreational, it might feel as though you've suddenly been dropped in the middle of France. Everything seems forbidding, unfamiliar and yet also kind of exotic. Oh, and you don't understand a word anyone is saying to you. However, as with a trip to Paris, once you get a handle on the language, the world of marijuana becomes a place you can more thoroughly enjoy, or at least navigate more easily.

To help novices who don't have a Master's degree in biology or a college roommate who sold weed to pay the rent, we asked noted cannabis industry educator and consultant Emma Chasen to provide definitions for some of the most common terms you'll need to know if you want to explore marijuana. Here they are.

Bud
The flower of the marijuana plant; it is used for recreational and medicinal purposes, since it contains the highest concentrations of active cannabinoids.

Budtenders
Dispensary employees who serve a function like pharmacists, answering questions and offering suggestions on products and strains based on customers' needs.

Cannabinoids
The chemical compounds in cannabis that act on the human body's cannabinoid receptors, producing various effects.

11-HYDROXY-THC
The form of THC that is made when delta-9-THC is orally ingested and gets processed through the liver. Smaller in size, 11-hydroxy-THC binds more efficiently to receptors and therefore exhibits very strong psychotropic activity. This explains why edibles can be so strong.

▶ BHO (BUTANE HASH OIL)
A common cannabis oil made using high heat/pressure. Usually dabbed.

Use of butane hash oil isn't new, but it's gaining popularity.

▲ BONG
A large pipe, usually made of glass, that uses water to diffuse and cool the smoke as you breathe it in.

BUBBLER
A handheld marijuana pipe, often glass, with a water reservoir to cool the smoke before it's inhaled.

Cannabis plants have been known to grow as high as 16 feet in some regions.

8

CANNABIS
The genus of the plant family Cannabaceae. This genus includes three species of flowering plants: sativa and indica (medical and adult-use marijuana) and ruderalis (naturally lower in THC).

9

CANNABIS INDICA
A cannabis plant species with distinct morphological characteristics, which grows short and bushy, produces dense, compact female flowers and is of the broad-leaf variety. It produces relaxing, almost sedative, physical effects.

10

CANNABIS RUDERALIS
A cannabis plant species with distinct morphological characteristics. It's found largely in rural, mountainous areas and does not produce many flowers or secondary compounds.

11

CANNABIS SATIVA
A cannabis plant species with distinct morphological characteristics, which grows tall and skinny, produces loose female flowers and is of the narrow-leaf variety. It produces more cerebral effects than the indica plant.

Infused butter, for cooking

12

CB1 & CB2 receptors
Cannabinoid receptors that are part of our endocannabinoid receptor system.

13

CBD (cannabidiol)
The second-most prominent cannabinoid found in the cannabis matrix. It's responsible for cannabis' many medicinal properties and is linked to anti-inflammatory, analgesic, anti-proliferative, anti-spasmodic and anxiolytic effects. It's a nonintoxicant.

14

CBG (cannabigerol)
The cannabinoid from which most other cannabinoids differentiate, referred to as a "stem-cell cannabinoid" and linked to many physiological properties, such as muscle relaxation and immune modulation as well as anti-inflammatory, anxiolytic and analgesic effects.

15

CBN (cannabinol)
The oxidative byproduct of THC. When THC is exposed to light and oxygen it degrades into CBN. CBN has anti-bacterial and sedative properties.

16

CO2
A common cannabis oil made using CO2 gas, high heat and high pressure. It's most often consumed vaporized.

17

Concentrates
A consolidation of cannabinoids created by dissolving marijuana into a solvent, resulting in products with high THC levels.

18

Dabbing
Heating cannabis concentrates and extracts at high temperatures to create a more potent effect.

A budtender will help you find the cannabis product that best fits your needs.

19

Dispensary, Access Point, Pickup Location
A licensed facility that follows state guidelines so patients and consumers can safely access cannabis.

20

DISTILLATE
A cannabis oil with a high concentration of one cannabinoid and a narrow range of additional compounds.

21

EDIBLES
Foods infused with cannabis extracts.

22

ENDOGENOUS CANNABINOIDS
Cannabinoids that are made in the human body.

23

ENDOGENOUS CANNABINOID RECEPTOR SYSTEM
Comprised of cannabinoid receptors, this body system allows us to feel the effects from phytocannabinoids.

24

ENSEMBLE EFFECT
The theory that all compounds found in the cannabis matrix work synergistically to produce the most medically efficacious experience.

Buds need to be dried and cured before use.

25

FECO (FULL-EXTRACT CANNABIS OIL)
A high-potency full-flower extract made using organic, food-grade alcohol. It's a viscous oil, most often used to help those with cancer or seizure disorders.

26

FLAVONOIDS
Phenolic compounds that can induce changes in physiology and have antioxidant and antiproliferative properties. These are found in the cannabis matrix.

27

FULL SPECTRUM
A way to process cannabis that retains the plant's range and ratio of compounds in the final product.

HEMP

A subspecies of cannabis thought to be most closely related to Cannabis sativa. It produces a consistent chemotype and is CBD-dominant, with less than 0.3 percent THC. Hemp is federally legal in the United States. It can be used to make rope, paper, beauty/wellness products, CBD oil and a vast array of other products.

HYBRID

A plant whose genetics are a cross between one or more separate cannabis strains. These are usually purposely bred to blend preferred traits from different strains into a new plant.

CBD oil

ICE HASH

A cannabis product made by vigorously shaking cannabis in ice water. This results in trichome residue that can be dried and smoked.

ISOLATE

A cannabis product that contains a singular compound (typically THC or CBD).

KUSH

A popular phrase that refers to a type of cannabis plant from the Hindu Kush mountains of Afghanistan and Pakistan. The strains are indicas and produce a distinctive aroma that their large fan base has described as "earthy."

MARIJUANA

Female cannabis plant in which flowers contain a high percentage of cannabinoids and hold both medicinal and psychoactive properties.

Microdosing
Consuming a very small amount of cannabis to see how you feel before trying more.

Plants
Multicellular organisms that produce their own food in the process of photosynthesis.

Primary Compounds
Compounds found in a plant, including water, minerals and by-products of photosynthesis, that support its essential functions.

Phyto-Cannabinoids
Cannabinoids found in plants.

Pre-Rolls
Marijuana cigarettes or joints.

Pre-roll

The harvest time for cannabis can depend on the variety.

STRAIN

A specific variety of plant species developed to produce distinct traits. Strain names reflect the plant's appearance, traits or place of origin.

SYNERGISTIC RELATIONSHIP

When two or more compounds work together to maximize the overall experience.

TERPENES

The volatile essential oils found in plants and some insects. They are abundantly found in cannabis; they give cannabis its distinct smells and also correlate to physiological effects.

THC

(tetrahydrocannabinol) A cannabinoid found abundantly in cannabis. It's responsible for cannabis' primary psychoactive effects (the high). It is also linked to many medicinal properties, including anti-inflammatory, analgesic and anti-proliferative effects.

Tincture

A liquid extraction made by using glycerine, alcohol or oil as the solvent.

Topicals

Cannabis-infused lotions and oils that are applied to the skin. Even if they contain THC, they should not get you high.

Trichomes

Glandular structures that sit on the surface of the plant and hold the secondary compounds.

Vape Pen

A device shaped like a pen, consisting of a cartridge with a heating element that produces vapor from liquid containing cannabinoids, or dried material from cannabis, allowing the user to inhale the aerosol vapor.

Vaporization
Heating dried plant material at temperatures below those needed to achieve combustion.

THE KEYS TO CANNABIS

Marijuana and hemp may come from the same plant species, but they are very different in what they offer and how they are used. Grow your knowledge here.

Marijuana

Ingredient: THC

- Has psychoactive effects
- Stimulates receptors in the brain's pleasure center
- Releases higher-than-normal levels of dopamine
- Creates a high

Ingredient: CBD

- Nonintoxicant
- Stimulates receptors in the brain that regulate pain perception, anxiety and nausea
- Medical applications include as an anti-inflammatory and a pain reliever
- When together, THC amplifies CBD and CBD offsets THC. Thus their nickname: "the power couple"

Possible Side Effects

- Racing heart
- Short-term memory issues
- Loss of balance
- Paranoia

Both hemp and
marijuana have
medical uses.

15

Hemp

The real renaissance around hemp stems from its economic benefits, from seed to sale (building materials, textiles, fuel). However, there is loud and serious chatter around its CBD-rich therapeutic oil.

Ingredient: CBD

■ Nonpsychotropic

■ According to the U.S. Department of Health and Human Services, CBD is "a neuroprotectant and antioxidant"

■ Beneficial for treating inflammation, and autoimmune and neurodegenerative diseases

Possible Side Effects

■ Nausea

■ Fatigue

CBD Label Facts

There is some confusion about the differences between hemp oil, CBD oil, hemp extract and CBD extract, as well as full-spectrum and isolate CBD.

1 / HEMP OIL
Cold-pressed from the seed.

2 / CBD OIL
Extracted from the flowers. Some companies label CBD oil (extract) as hemp oil in order to navigate regulation. Look for the words *CBD, extract* or *hemp extract* on a label. The product should contain CBD, because the "extract" is from hemp flowers (where cannabinoids are produced).

3 / FULL-SPECTRUM CBD Contains CBD and other minor cannabinoids (may include THC).

4 / CBD ISOLATE Contains 99.9 percent CBD and no other cannabinoids.

Hemp plants produce flowers in many colors.

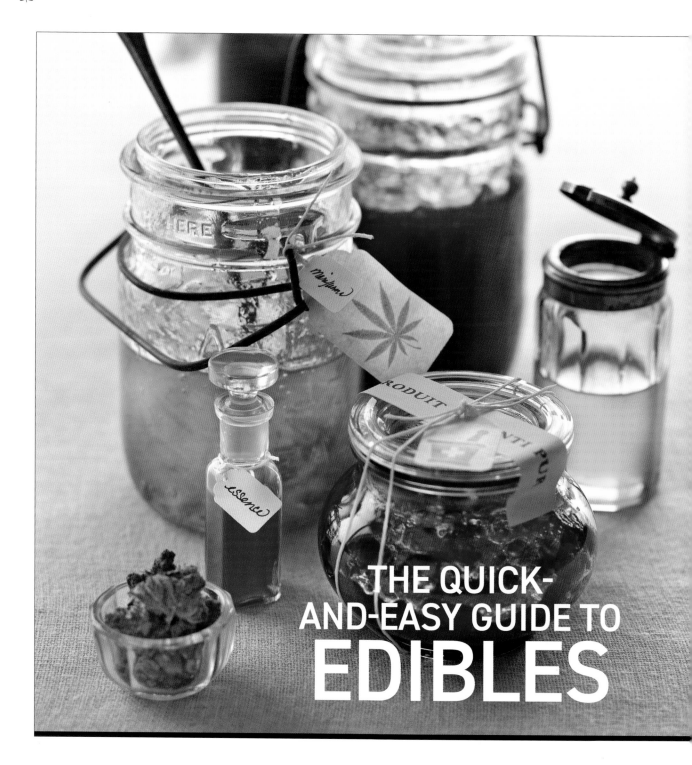

THE QUICK-AND-EASY GUIDE TO EDIBLES

16 THINGS YOU NEED TO KNOW

A PRIMER

①

Edibles

Foods or drinks, lozenges, tinctures, candies or mints infused with cannabis flower or concentrates.

②

The Benefits

Feel the effects without having to smoke or vape. Compared to other methods, edibles usually provide longer-lasting effects.

③

The Challenges

Timing or delayed onset. Since they're absorbed through the digestive system and metabolized through the liver, you may feel the effects within minutes—but they will most likely peak within an hour and then taper off at two hours.

④

HOW EDIBLES ARE MADE

Thanks to an interest in cannabis cuisine and the ability to isolate compounds like THC and CBD, edibles can be medicinal or recreational. When it comes to choosing an edible and anticipating the effects, it's important to know how it is made. Also, the ingredients and production process have an impact. In order to isolate the compounds into an oil for cooking, the process starts with separation via a solvent-based extraction process (hydrocarbon or CO_2) and then winterization (further refinement with ethanol), followed by decarboxylation (compounds are heated to activate medicinal properties). Finally, the material is run through a short-path steam-distillation or rational-distillation chamber to purify it. What remains: a translucent, viscous sap that resembles honey.

TERMS YOU NEED TO KNOW

⑤ SLANG
Includes space cakes, firecrackers or funny brownies. Two traditional Indian cannabis-infused drinks are bhang lassi and bhang thandai.

⑥ MARIJUANA-INFUSED BUTTER/OIL
The most common way for consumers to make their own edibles. Note: The process is time-consuming but worth it.

⑦ TINCTURE
A liquid cannabis extract. Tinctures can be flavored and are usually placed under the tongue (sublingual) with a dropper. They can also be mixed into a drink.

⑧ CRYSTALLINE
The purest form of cannabis concentrate, it includes a single cannabinoid. It can be sprinkled on food or blended with ingredients.

BYE-BYE, BONE-DRY POT BROWNIES (THANKS TO INFUSED BUTTER AND OIL).

⑨ FIND YOUR DOSE
Potency is indicated by the amount of cannabinoids in milligrams, per serving and in the full package.

Beginner
1mg–5mg
Best Practice
Tincture (easily dosed in a precise manner)

Some Experience
5mg–10mg
Best Practice
Baked goods (for an all-body high and relaxation)

Lots of Experience
10mg or more
Best Practice
Capsules (long-lasting, highly concentrated method)

BEFORE YOU CHOOSE, REMEMBER

10 The "right" dose varies between people. Everyone's internal footprint is different, based on such factors as previous cannabis use, hormones and sensitivities. (See "Find Your Dose," left.)

11 Listen to your body. Don't overdo it. Start small and add gradually. Consume at a measured pace.

12 If you don't feel any effects right away, don't take more. Wait. Keep in mind that it can take up to an hour to take effect. Edibles are absorbed through the digestive system, which results in a slower onset.

13 Tracking how you feel the first time will help you later on. A strain-and-health journal will let you know what works and what doesn't. You'll notice patterns that you can go over with your doctor in order to make modifications.

FAQS

14

Can I wash down my cookie with a beer?
It is not recommended to mix cannabis and alcohol. And if you are on any medications, check with your doctor before mixing in cannabis.

15

My best friend's sister made pot brownies. Should I?
You should...proceed with great caution—you have no idea about the ingredient amount or dosage. Start slow and low.

16

What if I take too much?
Your body could react (nausea, dizziness). Stop, drop and roll into bed. Breathe deeply, drink water and sleep it off. It will wear off...eventually; take it from emergency-room doctors, who tend to simply watch over patients until the effects wear off.

A growing number of the canna-curious try edibles to improve their health, not to get high.

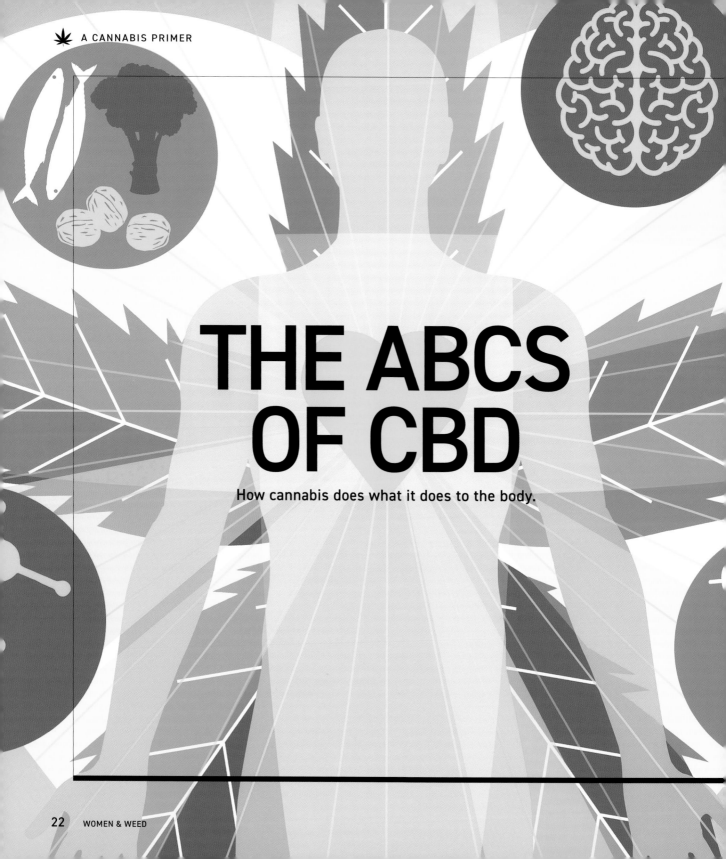

THE ABCS
OF CBD

How cannabis does what it does to the body.

To understand how and why medical marijuana does what it does to you when you ingest it, you have to first imagine your body as sort of a walking cellphone network. The human body is filled with millions of receptors, and for you to feel anything —pain or pleasure or something in between—those neurotransmitters need to talk to each other constantly.

"They have to tell each other what's going on and then allow it to happen," says Emma Chasen, director of education for the Sativa Science Club, a website designed to monitor the cannabis industry by providing instruction and networking opportunities. "Picture it as if one of your cells is calling the next one over, saying you need to make this or that change."

Now, somewhere within all these chatty cells is what scientists have identified as the endocannabinoid system (ECS). Named after Cannabis sativa, the breed of the plant that produces marijuana's mental and physical sensations, it has receptors that affect everything we think, feel and do. Which brings us to CBD (cannabidiol) and THC (tetrahydrocannabinol), the two most prominent chemicals found in cannabis.

When eaten, smoked, vaped or rubbed on your aching knee, those chemicals traipse through your bloodstream into your brain. THC, which is the most common cannabinoid in the marijuana plant, provides marijuana's psychoactive effects because it specifically stimulates the aforementioned receptors that exist in your brain's pleasure center. In turn, that releases a larger-than-normal level of the chemical dopamine—hence, your "high."

Then there's CBD, which is the second-most prominent cannabis compound and is considered a nonintoxicant. So when you consume high-CBD products like oils or edibles, it connects with a variety of brain receptors and offers something perhaps a bit more soothing than THC.

Explains Chasen, "It has a variety of medicinal properties. It is anti-inflammatory, anti-anxiety, antispasmodic. It's really helpful with neurotherapy, because it can connect with opioid receptors in the body and allow them to, in a sense, widen. It makes the body feel more of the effect from the opioids we make with our physiology."

CBD IS THE TRUE MVP

As medical marijuana increases in popularity, CBD is starting to seem like the plant's MVP. Thanks to more research and lots of Grateful Dead concerts, THC has always gotten more of the attention—and it does have some medicinal value. With the right dosage, it can be "powerful in fighting cancer and as an anti-anxiety agent," says Chasen. Meanwhile, CBD can promote some psychoactive reactions, but even that is more comforting than intoxicating for medical marijuana patients. "It can give you a 'body high,' like when you sit in a hot tub and come out with your muscles super-relaxed—but [you're] not high," she explains. "There's a change in your physiology, but you can still drive and work and engage." Read on for more about how CBD can impact your health.

> ❝
> **MEDICAL MARIJUANA CAN BE POWERFUL IN FIGHTING CANCER AND AS AN ANTI-ANXIETY AGENT."**
>
> **EMMA CHASEN**
> **CANNABIS EDUCATOR**

The only conclusive evidence of CBD's healing potential is its anti-spasmodic ability.

Q There's so much discussion of CBD now, but what exactly is it?
CBD is an abbreviation for cannabidiol, one of more than 100 identified molecules in hemp and cannabis plants, according to Anna Symonds, director of the Oregon-based educational organization CBD Certified. Although people have spent thousands of years using the entire cannabis plant for both its medicinal and mind-altering effects, it wasn't until the 1960s that Israeli scientist Dr. Raphael Mechoulam became the first to map and describe the structure of the CBD molecule.

Q The stories about CBD all seem pretty miraculous, but what are some issues that it can help me with?
First, it's important to remember that scientists have yet to prove very much when it comes to CBD's healing powers. Explains Symonds, "We need much more research and more clinical trials." However, veteran cannabis industry educator/consultant Emma Chasen notes that there has been conclusive evidence regarding CBD's anti-spasmodic and anti-epileptic abilities. In addition, preclinical studies have found CBD may also be an anti-inflammatory, an analgesic, a muscle relaxer, an antidepressant and an immunity modulator. Meanwhile, there's plenty of anecdotal evidence that it

has helped sufferers of everything from psoriasis to anorexia to insomnia to Parkinson's.

Q Is there a difference between a hemp plant and a cannabis plant when it comes to buying CBD?
Yes, although they are closely related. "Hemp is a kissing cousin of the cannabis plant," says Shira Adler, author and founder of Synergy by Shira Adler. Morris Beegle, president of the Colorado Hemp Company and founder of the NoCo Hemp Expo, the world's largest hemp conference and exhibition, admits telling the difference between the two can be confusing, since "hemp is one molecule compound away from the cannabis plant." For cannabis to be considered hemp, it legally has to have less than 0.3 percent of the intoxicating cannabinoid THC. This essentially means hemp-based CBD, which is legal across the country, is more like a vitamin than a medicine, while "the CBD in dispensaries in legal states comes from the cannabis side," Beegle explains.

Holding CBD oil under the tongue will allow it to be absorbed directly into the bloodstream.

Q It seems almost too good to be true. So how does it work when we consume it?
Every part of us—from our brains to our internal organs to our respiratory and muscular systems—has what are called CBD receptors. These soak up the CBD, which Adler says "just knows what is out of whack. It addresses your deficiency points and what is causing them." CBD is "a very promiscuous compound," adds Chasen. "It can interact with many different receptor families and factors in the body, initiating a variety of physiological responses, all with the goal of maintaining homeostasis [a state of equilibrium within the body]."

Q When using a medicine that's strictly CBD, will I be able to avoid getting "high"?
Completely. It doesn't have the same intoxication properties that THC does. However, people wrongly assume that CBD is "non-psychoactive," says Symonds. "While it's nonintoxicating, it is in fact psychoactive—it interacts with our nervous system to produce changes in mood and/or behavior, including anti-anxiety and anti-psychotic [symptoms]. So it won't get you high, but it's a good thing that it's psychoactive, because we can gain therapeutic effects through these pathways."

WHAT YOU SHOULD KNOW

Get the facts before you go out and spend your money.

CBD (cannabidiol), a cannabis compound with medical benefits:
- Is nonintoxicating—it does not make you feel stoned
- Is (possibly) able to counteract the psychoactivity of THC
- Is a natural anti-inflammatory, a strong anti-oxidant, an anti-depressant and a neuroprotector
- Is an option for people looking for relief from inflammation, pain and anxiety

Where does it come from? Mainly from the leaves, resin or flowering tops, but not the stems, of cannabis plants.

How is it extracted? Cannabis oil should be extracted without toxic solvents and formulated with no artificial ingredients, chemical preservatives, thinning agents or corn syrup. A common practice uses carbon dioxide (CO2) under high pressure and extremely low temperatures to isolate the oil.

How does it work? The body produces endocannabinoids, neurotransmitters that bind to cannabinoid receptors in the nervous system. CBD can reduce pain by impacting endocannabinoid receptor activity, reducing inflammation and interacting with neurotransmitters.

The great debate: hemp-derived vs. marijuana-derived CBD Cultivators are now developing high-resin, CBD-rich varieties with less than 0.3% THC —the legal limit—so the great debate is no longer an issue. Until these strains are more widespread, look for CBD derived from high-resin plants with strong terpenes.

Watch out for unsubstantiated claims The FDA dinged a number of companies selling CBD that claimed it could cure or reverse cancer. The agency has approved only one marijuana-based drug, Epidiolex, that contains a form of cannabidiol that is used to treat Lennox-Gastaut syndrome and Dravet syndrome, which are forms of epilepsy.

The difference between CBD-rich and CBD-dominant strains
CBD-RICH a strain or product that has equal amounts of CBD and THC, or more CBD than THC.
CBD-DOMINANT a strain or product that is rich in CBD but has very little THC content.

Possible side effects of CBD Nausea, fatigue and diarrhea

Label facts
HEMP OIL cold-pressed from the seed
CBD OIL extracted from the flowers
FULL-SPECTRUM contains CBD and other minor cannabinoids (maybe THC)
CBD ISOLATE contains 99.9% CBD and no other cannabinoids

Don't be afraid:
- To find out about the CBD supply chain from seed to sale, since the market is unregulated
- To ask a company for lab-test reports (Certificates of Analysis or COAs)
- To choose companies that use American-grown hemp. (Note: States with legalized cannabis laws have stricter standards.)

Delivery options (in order of effectiveness)
VAPE PENS inhaled CBD tends to enter the bloodstream faster than other forms—but make sure the pen is solvent-free and be mindful of dosage/inhale/draw.
TINCTURES Drops or sprays are the next in line and can be effective under the tongue (hold for 30 seconds before swallowing) or sprayed inside the cheeks.
TOPICAL Rub creams or oils on sore muscles or inflammation for relief.
EDIBLE If you consume food or drink infused with CBD, the CBD takes longer to take effect, since the food/drink needs to be absorbed by the body.

SEEDING IS BELIEVING

Hemp seed oil isn't CBD, but it can still be helpful.

As the CBD phenomenon continues to flourish, it's hard enough for consumers to learn the difference between hemp-derived CBD oils and cannabis-derived CBD oils. To make it even more confusing, though, many companies have also stepped up the marketing of what they call "hemp seed oil." So what's the difference between all of these treatments? Cannabis educator/consultant Emma Chasen explains it this way: "Hemp-derived CBD products can be efficacious in managing a variety of symptoms. However, it's very important to examine the source of hemp and the product formulation practices. Cannabis-derived CBD may be the most efficacious in managing symptoms, due to the rigorous analytical testing requirements. Hemp seed oil does not contain CBD, so it will not have much therapeutic potential."

Still, that doesn't mean it's without any healing powers. "Hemp seed oil is generally recognized as something safe to take, like echinacea or lavender," says Morris Beegle, president of the Colorado Hemp Company and founder of the NoCo Hemp Expo. "The seeds have a lot of nutritional value, like flax or chia seeds...very high in protein and omegas 3, 6 and 9. Humans have been eating them for a long time, probably thousands of years, long before we knew what CBD was."

The CBD molecule is called "promiscuous" because it works through multiple pathways.

AS YOU LIKE IT

When it comes to CBD consumption, there are many options to suit your needs.

There's no doubt we live in an era of seemingly unlimited choices. Whether you're looking for a TV show to watch, someone to deliver your Chinese food or a cellular company to keep you connected with Wi-Fi, you can easily get overwhelmed with service options. CBD is no different. There was a time when cannabis was simply that funny-smelling stuff you smoked, or your roommate's hippie friend baked into brownies. As interest in cannabidiol increases, though, so do the methods for consuming it. Here is a look at both the benefits and the drawbacks of the most popular ways to indulge.

SMOKING

Once the only game in town, it's still a popular way to get high—if that's your goal. However, if you're more interested in the healing effects of CBD than the intoxicating effects of THC, smoking is the wrong move. According to Jim Walsh, a veteran cannabis public relations specialist whose clients include industry leader Bloom Farms, very little marijuana flower in the U.S. has much CBD. That means "there are much better ways to go at this stage if CBD is what you want," he explains.

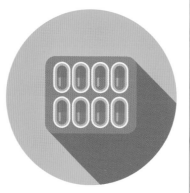

SUPPLEMENTS

These "aren't that common right now, but they're getting there," explains Walsh. They are like a multivitamin for the new cannabis era, providing a synergistic effect by combining CBD with other healthy ingredients. These "cocktails of things that are beneficial for people," Walsh adds, will most likely have the same onset time as an edible, since they go through the same route in the body. However, "these are still very new, so it's hard to say. That's why it's important to buy them from a reputable brand you already trust."

EDIBLES

Whether it's in a gummy bear, a cookie or a chocolate bar, eating your CBD is fast becoming the most popular form of consumption. Still, it must pass through your liver before it can head off to do its thing, which can mean an onset time of between 20 minutes and two hours, explains Walsh. However, once it does get going, the CBD can work for up to four or five hours. "This can lead to a common error," Walsh says. "People take a little, think it's not working, then take more—which you shouldn't do."

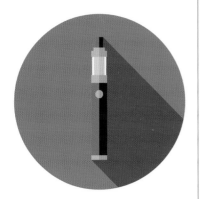

VAPING

This can be done in two different ways: with a vape pen, or a larger vaporizer (picture that thing your mom used to put in your room when you had a bad cold). The primary benefit with vaping is the rapid onset of the effects, which can hit you in as few as five minutes. The downsides? Walsh says it can be hard to find a pen that effectively delivers CBD and the effect usually fades within 90 minutes. And concern about vaping-related illnesses has led many to stop using the method altogether.

TOPICALS

Think lotions, creams, salves and bath bombs, all of which are gaining in popularity these days. The CBD in these treatments can start having an effect in five to 15 minutes in many cases, because the topicals are usually being applied to the precise location where you need help. That's great news for people dealing with conditions involving inflammation, such as fibromyalgia and rheumatoid arthritis. However, adds Walsh, the skin will absorb some of the product, possibly limiting CBD's ability to fully treat patients.

INGESTIBLES

This includes tinctures—drops you put under your tongue—and sublinguals—things like mints that you hold in your mouth as they dissolve. Both can quickly move into your bloodstream. The onset time from a tincture dropper, according to Walsh, can be around 30 minutes, with the effects lasting about as long as an edible. Sublinguals, meanwhile, could possibly get to work within seven to 10 minutes. "[Ingestibles] offer some level of consistency in dosing," says Walsh. "That's what I personally like about them."

THE NOSE KNOWS

Terpenes, essential oils and aromatherapy have medical benefits. Cannabis has high levels of terpenes (up to 200 different aromatic oils that give each strain its individual fragrance and taste), all of which work together to give the plant its unique aromas and effects. Ocimene, citrusy, with anti-inflammatory and antifungal properties; and guaiol, piney, with antimicrobial properties, are common.

Why terpenes matter
- They synergize with cannabis compounds.
- They have medical benefits and are best used in whole-plant therapies with other compounds.
- They give cannabis its flavor.

Cannabis contains terpenes that are also found in other plants and fruits, such as...
- Limonene, found in citrus; treats acid reflux, anxiety and depression
- Myrcene, found in hops; has sedative effects and is also a sleep aid and muscle relaxer
- Beta-caryophyllene, found in black pepper; is an anti-inflammatory and analgesic and protects the cells lining the digestive tract

You can combine cannabis with essential oils to enhance or moderate its effects. You can even create new effects for a customized experience that targets a specific health issue.

Hemp activist
Dani Billings
is on a mission to
save the planet
with this crop.

THE YEAR
OF HEMP

Everything you need to know about the current state of
the plant that's been around for thousands of years.

Every five years or so, Congress passes a farm bill, a legislation package that governs food and farm systems. It speaks to how and what kinds of foods are grown. It covers programs from crop insurance to healthy food access. It fosters rural development as well as research and conservation. Most recently, the $867 billion Agricultural Improvement Act of 2018—aka the Farm Bill—was passed. But among the nutrition, crop-insurance, conservation and commodity programs was one big change: legalizing hemp.

Hemp has been around for thousands of years, and both Presidents George Washington and Thomas Jefferson grew the crop. The trouble began when Congress passed the Marihuana Tax Act 1937. While marijuana and hemp both derive from Cannabis sativa, they are distinct strains with unique phytochemical compositions. But when they were lumped together in the bill, hemp prohibition began.

Recently, hemp has gained renewed mainstream interest because of its reputation as a sustainable wonder crop. Yet for years, and despite its legal murkiness, many farmers and people have believed in the plant and its uses, from textiles to food to building materials to medicine, just to name a few. One of these people is Dani Billings—and you may not know it from looking at her, but Billings has been working with the plant for years. Despite her youthful look, she has procured seed, farmed hemp (in partnerships with hundreds of farms in the U.S., Mexico and Jamaica), processed and extracted oils, formulated recipes and seen hundreds of patients— not to mention promoting hempcrete domes, waste and recycle management systems, and textiles. Billings is in demand as a consultant and healer. She travels throughout the world, speaking on behalf of the plant and her work.

In reality, Billings is a Denver girl, the daughter of a farmer and a holistic nutritionist and the mother of a 10-year-old son. These are the people who make up her inner circle and keep her going. "Bill, my dad, is just an OG, a farm-logistics guy, a socializer, a hustler who is helping to give back to the farmers he has worked with for years. He tells you how it is and really is just the best guy ever." Her mother, Tracee, is her go-to for questions about plant medicine, nutrition and how the body works. And then there is her son, who cannot decide whether he wants to become a professional athlete or a hemp farmer. "I am educating my son, who has been around the plant his whole life, with the truth. He has been on hemp farms since he could walk. He is the future."

IN THE BEGINNING...

Before Billings was in demand and a social media presence, she was a teenager in the city—the plant was at the forefront of her mind, and she was inspired by its possibilities. In 2008, when Colorado legalized medical marijuana, Billings started a mom-and-pop edibles business called Tastee Yummees. It launched her career, creating a cannabis network, and Billings began to feel complete and fulfilled, helping people, educating patients and nourishing the Earth. "I was called to do this," she repeats over and over again.

It wasn't always easy. "It was a rough industry between 2008 and 2011," she recalls. "It was just the

Hemp farms are just beginning to take seed.

supply chain. She opened an extraction lab and worked with private and white-label clients; Billings also plans to open a paper and plastics facility that will turn cannabis waste into a variety of products.

BEYOND CBD

Many see hemp's biggest growth potential as coming from hemp-derived cannabidiol (CBD), which is used in medical, health and wellness products. And it is true that prior to legalization, hemp-derived CBD, which had been operating in a legal gray area, had grown into a $600 million industry. Billings chooses to focus on the whole plant, with an emphasis on sustainability and innovation and new pathways as well as CBD. "People can get stuck on CBD—but it's not the only compound within the plant, nor is it the only use," she says. "The plant has more to offer and needs to be promoted and studied, and people need to be educated."

This is what led Billings to Arizona and the Veteran Village Kins Community. The holistic healing and learning center that supports veterans with PTSD and addictions is situated on a 2.5-acre lot that is designed to be self-sustaining, with 1 acre allocated to growing hemp. Ten companies, including Billings',

beginning of the Wild West, with hustlers, guns and meetings in random buildings." Before more formal regulations came in 2012, Billings had been robbed so many times, from production product to actual money, that she sold her recipes and stepped back. But not for long. Suddenly, hemp became legal in Colorado—and with her connections to seed collections, she couldn't resist the call. Billings developed the first successful legal hemp farm. Word got out, and she quickly expanded to help build farms in several other legal states, a partnership

farm in Jamaica and, starting in 2019, in Mexico and New Zealand.

In 2014, Billings heard the call from people and patients again and developed Nature's Root, a line of body-care products with CBD as well as hemp seed oil, which acts as an anti-inflammatory and moisturizer. And it wasn't long before Nature's Root Spa opened in Jamaica, in conjunction with the dispensary Kaya (another one is scheduled to open outside Denver).

But Billings did not stop there; she decided to vertically integrate to protect herself throughout the have been working together to build solar and wind power, develop organic vegetable farms, and teach veterans how to farm hemp and build with it. "The Colorado Hemp Project and Hemp Inc. have been working together to build hemp domes," says Billings, "housing that is built by the crops on the land. The 2,000-square-foot domes are made from a similar product to hempcrete but infused with air so they are lighter and stronger."

Next up: Hemp Haven, an open ranch/resort. "I want to create multiple havens around the world for people to live, build and give back. It's all about sustainability."

THE CALL OF CANNABIS

No matter where hemp may take Billings, she always thinks about one of her first patients, Terry, who reached out through a phone number printed on the back of the packaging of her original edibles. Terry, who had stage 4 stomach cancer and a brain tumor, found the edible cappuccino crisp the only thing that would help her sleep. "We met, and it was as if we had known each other forever," recalls Billings, who immediately consulted with her mom to create a new, sugar-free version. She began making specific edibles for Terry; when she could no longer eat, Billings brought her some of the first-ever CO2 medical-marijuana oil. "I believed that saved her life," says Billings. "She put it in tea or swabbed it in her mouth. It was Blue Dream oil, with a specific terpene and cannabinoid profile, THC and other CB compounds. The mixture, together with the fats, lipids and low waxes to help bind product to receptors, helped Terry beat [her cancer]. It's the whole plant. It always comes back to the whole plant."

FOUR THINGS TO KNOW ABOUT THE 2018 FARM BILL
(courtesy of NORML, The National Organization for the Reform of Marijuana Laws)

1

The hemp-specific provisions amend the federal Controlled Substances Act so that hemp plants containing no more than 0.3 percent THC are not classified as Schedule I controlled substances under federal law.

2

The Act broadens the definition of hemp to include "any part of the plant, including extracts [or] cannabinoids" that do not possess greater than 0.3 percent THC on a dry-weight basis.

3

The Act permits states that wish to possess "primary regulatory authority over the production of hemp" to submit a plan to the U.S. Secretary of Agriculture. The agency has 60 days to approve, disapprove or amend it. In instances where a state-proposed plan is not approved, "it shall be unlawful to produce hemp in that state...without a license." Federal-grant opportunities will be available to licensed commercial farmers, as will the ability for farmers to obtain crop insurance. The Act doesn't federally recognize nonlicensed, noncommercial hemp activities.

4

Nothing in the new language will "affect or modify" the existing regulatory powers of the U.S. FDA or other agencies with regard to the enforcement of the U.S. Food, Drugs and Cosmetics Act or the Public Health Service Act.

SORRY—THERE WAS ONLY ONE MADE!

The car contained solar panels in its roof.

HEMP VS. FIBERGLASS
Way back in 2008, hemp was used in the body panels, rear spoiler and seats of the Lotus Eco Elise car. Hemp is stronger, lighter and cheaper than fiberglass—and is beautiful to look at.

CBD oil is just one of the many outputs of the plant.

THE FDA AND HEMP

After the Agriculture Improvement Act of 2018 became law, FDA Commissioner Scott Gottlieb restated the FDA's stance: CBD is a drug ingredient and illegal to add to food or health products without approval from the agency. "Selling unapproved products with unsubstantiated therapeutic claims is not only a violation of the law but also can put patients at risk, as these products have not been proven to be safe or effective," Gottlieb wrote. However, an FDA-approved drug for the treatment of seizures—Epidiolex—contains cannabis-derived CBD.

The FDA stated that three ingredients derived from hemp—hulled hemp seeds, hemp seed protein and hemp seed oil—are safe as foods and won't require additional approvals, so long as marketers do not make claims that they treat disease.

DELIVER US UNTO HEMP-NATION

A short history of medical marijuana.

Nearly 160 million people worldwide reportedly consume some form of marijuana.

Pollen from cannabis was found on the mummy of Ramesses II, who died in 1213 B.C.

T hey say that those who don't know history are doomed to repeat it. If that's indeed true, the 93 percent of Americans who support medical marijuana might want to learn the history of hemp.

For centuries, the plant was widely regarded as beneficial for one's health, but eventually Cannabis sativa (aka marijuana) found itself on the frontline in the war on drugs. These days, it's back in vogue, with 33 states and the District of Columbia having established some sort of medical-cannabis program. But how long will this pro-pot trend last? To get a sense of that future, here's a look at medical marijuana's past.

2700s B.C.-1500s A.D.

IN THE BEGINNING...
From malaria to constipation, hemp helped early human health.

Think of hemp as the Swiss Army knife of agriculture. From the first moment it was harvested, which could have been as long ago as 10,000 years, it was a truly multipurpose plant that helped a little with a lot of things. For instance, it could be used for rope, for clothes, for paper and for food.

"Hemp was a major part of the world economy for the past several thousand years," explains Gooey Rabinski, author of *Understanding Medical Marijuana*. "It was primarily used at first for industrial materials, not really for medical needs."

Cannabis Crosses Continents
As far as researchers can tell, the first medical use was documented around 2700 B.C., when Chinese Emperor Shen Neng apparently prescribed a marijuana-based tea for maladies ranging from malaria to constipation to memory loss. By 1200 B.C., the Egyptians were reportedly using cannabis for glaucoma and in enemas. Meanwhile, in India, a blend of cannabis was seen as a cure for leprosy and, when mixed with milk, an anesthetic.

The cannabis used was a far cry from the version in the 20th century, when people discovered the euphoria the plant's THC could provide. But there's no doubt about its popularity as medicine by the time of the Middle Ages. "It's widely known that in countries like India, Pakistan and others, cannabis was used for thousands of years," says John Hudak, a senior fellow at the Brookings Institution and the author of *Marijuana: A Short History*. "It's safe to say that historically, people have really not been afraid of this product."

1600s

CANNABIS GOES CONTINENTAL

Medical hemp was transported around the globe; it's also rumored that even the Bard of Avon partook of the bud.

Whether it was silk, spices or the *Kama Sutra*, there were very few things from Eastern culture that didn't make their way to Europe as trade routes expanded and explorers began to travel the globe. So it comes as no surprise that by the 1600s, cannabis had arrived on the continent.

English clergyman and Oxford scholar Robert Burton recommended cannabis in his 1621 book *The Anatomy of Melancholy* as a treatment for depression. And, according to a report in the *South African Journal Of Science*, it's very possible that William Shakespeare himself smoked the occasional cannabis flower as a stimulant.

By the time England was sending settlers across the ocean to colonize what would become America, says Rabinski, "people in Europe were getting hip to the medical efficacy of cannabis. I've heard they even recommended cannabis tea for the queen. It wasn't the modern cannabis we know today, where we've taken female hemp plants and bred them to increase the THC levels, but it was definitely popular."

1700s

COMING TO AMERICA

When colonists arrived, they didn't just bring a desire for freedom; they brought hemp. Lots of hemp.

British colonists arrived on America's shores with more than a desire to build a new home. They also arrived with bags of hemp seed. Explains Hudak, "The plant provided a versatile crop, a cash crop. It could be used to create ...a number of things that were important to the British government. So, during colonial rule, citizens were required by the Crown to grow hemp. And even later, when they were no longer required to do so, colonial landowners recognized the value of the plant." Even the Founding Fathers, like George Washington and Thomas Jefferson, were hemp growers. There are claims that they were breeding the plant to increase THC levels for recreational consumption, but Rabinski's research has proven otherwise. However, there are writings from colonial days concerning both the plant's possible intoxicating and medical attributes, even, reportedly, from John Adams (though under a pseudonym). "It's not crystal clear whether it was used medicinally in terms of its intoxicating effects," Hudak says. "There were discussions around those effects, and it was surely something farmers stumbled upon. It's important to remember that at that time, farmers weren't purists. They loved getting drunk, and opium was big—so it's not far-fetched to think that they were using it as an intoxicant, even though that wasn't its primary purpose."

Traveling salesmen hawked "health tonics" that included cannabis.

1800s

TAKING OUR MEDICINE

As word of cannabis' potential powers began to spread, it may even have been used to ease some royal pains.

Through much of the 1800s, according to Hudak, "cannabis products were available all across the country for medicinal use." However, when it came to healing, America was also what Rabinski refers to as a "do-it-yourself medical culture." If you were sick, you popped down to the local apothecary shop to see what oils, ointments, lozenges, creams and candies it had to cure you.

And thanks in part to Sir William O'Shaughnessy, an Irish doctor who had served in India, many of those items contained some cannabis. While in India, he'd studied Eastern medicine and brought many of the ideas he'd discovered to England in the 1840s. That included recommending a particular Cannabis sativa strain for cholera patients. Meanwhile, Queen Victoria was so convinced of its healing powers, she reportedly used cannabis to ease the pain of menstrual cramps.

Says Hudak, "I can't say exactly what impact [O'Shaughnessy's] work ultimately had, but it did make cannabis as medicine more acceptable, because Americans and Britons were more likely to believe something written by a guy named O'Shaughnessy than by someone with an Indian name."

Queen Victoria

Sir William O'Shaughnessy

Finding Acceptance

By 1850, cannabis was listed in the *United States Pharmacopeia*, the official authority for all prescription and over-the-counter medicines. It was suggested as a treatment for a range of ailments, including gout, tonsillitis, anthrax, uterine bleeding, alcoholism, insanity and incontinence. However, according to Rabinski, cannabis had fallen out of favor by the dawn of the 20th century. Not only were more reliable medications, like aspirin, being created, but the invention of the hypodermic needle allowed treatments to be injected directly.

A still from 1936's *Reefer Madness*, which fueled anti-drug sentiment.

REEFER SADNESS

Thanks to racism and bad press, marijuana fell from favor.

The beginning of the end of cannabis' golden era can be traced directly back to 1906, when the Pure Food and Drug Act was signed into law. It was, says Hudak, "an effort by progressives to standardize and bring product-safety standards to medicine and food." The law wasn't specifically aimed at cannabis—but at the same time, the drug was falling from favor, thanks to its association with immigration. Mexicans fleeing civil war in their country were coming into America, and they brought their breed of cannabis—"marihuana"—with them. As U.S. citizens worried about this influx of immigrants from south of the border, the drug became what Hudak refers to as "a proxy for racism." People feared the arrival of Mexicans in their towns and associated marijuana with that paranoia. As a result, cities and states began to ban the drug entirely, regardless of any medical benefits.

A Taxing Situation

By the mid-1930s, marijuana had also been adopted by the jazz culture and was widely regarded (at least by white America) as a cause of everything from crime to mental illness, courtesy of stories spread in William Randolph Hearst's newspapers and from propaganda films like 1936's *Reefer Madness*. So, spurred on by Harry Anslinger, the first commissioner of the Federal Bureau of Narcotics, Congress passed the Marihuana Tax Act Of 1937.

The law required that all purchases of cannabis from any medical entity get a tax stamp from the U.S. Treasury in order to be certified. The American Medical Association opposed the legislation, claiming marijuana was still an "unknown quantity but might have important uses in medicine and psychology." Nonetheless, the Tax Act became law, with the Treasury

GOING TO CALIFORNIA How the Golden State's 1996 law changed the game.

From surf music to sourdough bread to Valley girls, California has long been responsible for some significant trends in American culture. Few have been as noteworthy, though, as the trend toward legalizing medical marijuana. The movement can be dated back to 1996 and California's Compassionate Use Act. Passed by a 56 percent majority vote on November 5, 1996, Proposition 215 was a ballot initiative that exempted patients and caregivers who possessed or grew marijuana for doctor-recommended medical treatments from criminal prosecution.

Although it was derided by politicians at the time—California Sen. Dianne Feinstein complained that the law would allow people "to drive a truckload of marijuana through the holes in it"—the measure was "the first big victory of the modern marijuana reform movement," says Tom Angell, chairman of the cannabis-advocacy group Marijuana Majority. "The voters of the country's most populous state dealt a big blow to overarching federal prohibition with Proposition 215."

Gooey Rabinski, author of *Understanding Medical Marijuana*, adds additional insight: "It got people's attention when a state with the sixth-largest GDP in the world passed a law regulating medical marijuana for 30-some million people."

The law wasn't perfect, but, according to Angell, it provided a framework to show the world "what a regulated medical-marijuana market looks like." And there's been no turning back.

"There was certainly the prominent stereotype at the time that people who consume marijuana are just silly, forgetful stoners who get the munchies," says Angell. "With the victory in California, and with the states that followed, that [image] has been undermined."

refusing to pass out the required tax stamps, according to Hudak. So for all intents and purposes, marijuana was illegal and could no longer be used for legitimate medical concerns.

1970s

WAGING A WEED WAR

Despite reports to the contrary, a president turned marijuana into a public enemy.

Once the U.S. government decided to treat all marijuana as evil, it became the unofficial mascot of 1960s counterculture, a rebellion you could inhale. The more hippies smoked it, the more the government hated it. "Because cannabis was illegal, using it became a way of flipping the middle finger at the establishment," says Rabinski. So in 1970, Congress passed the Controlled Substances Act—and enshrined marijuana as a menace to the country with a Schedule 1 designation (see sidebar, pg 49).

Drawing Battle Lines

Two years later, the National Commission on Marihuana and Drug Abuse released the report "Marihuana: A Signal of Misunderstanding." The study had been commissioned by

In 1969, as pot became a hippie staple, only 4 percent of U.S. adults said they had tried it.

President Richard Nixon, who was so unhappy with its suggestion to legalize marijuana that "he called the head of the commission (former Pennsylvania Governor Raymond Shafer) and told him to scrap the report," says Hudak. "When Shafer refused, Nixon went public with his criticism and started the 'war on drugs.'"

Adds Rabinski, "At the time, average Americans believed what they were told. If Nixon said dirty hippies were ruining the country with their damn music and their damn weed, people agreed. And the memory of medical use was wiped away."

1980s-2000s

A BUDDING MOVEMENT

A president just said no—but after a major health crisis, America said yes to medical marijuana.

The war on drugs had a new field general in the 1980s: President Ronald Reagan, who—along with his wife, Nancy—promoted marijuana abstinence with their Just Say No campaign. And for those who couldn't say no, he signed the Anti-Drug Abuse Act of 1986 into law. Penalties were now so severe that someone could get the same prison sentence for possessing 100 marijuana plants as they would for possessing 100 grams of heroin.

An Epidemic Becomes a Movement

Despite the stiff penalties, though, there was still a "thriving black market for marijuana, with millions of tons being grown and transported," explains Rabinski. A lot of that cannabis was flowing to victims of the AIDS epidemic, who were turning en masse to cannabis for help with their pain and suffering. This created a movement that resulted in Proposition P in San Francisco, a 1991 initiative that called on California lawmakers to legalize and add "hemp medical preparations" to the list of available treatments for patients. Five years later, California voters passed Proposition 215, allowing the use of

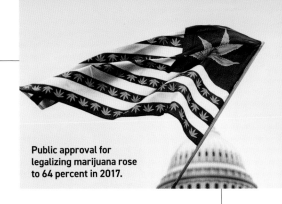

Public approval for legalizing marijuana rose to 64 percent in 2017.

marijuana for a variety of illnesses.

Five years after that, in 2001, Canada authorized a federal medical-marijuana program that Rabinski calls "the first of its kind—and really amazing because an entire country has done this. And that inspired a lot of activists on the medical and adult-use fronts to do what they're doing now. And the tide is turning, thanks to all these voter initiatives we're seeing across the country."

WHAT IS A SCHEDULE 1 DRUG? A 1970 law is keeping medical marijuana illegal today.

With every passing year, support for medical marijuana increases across the country. No matter how popular those laws become, though, there is one thing keeping medicinal cannabis from becoming legal nationwide: Schedule 1—the federal rule that bans its use.

In 1970, Congress passed the Controlled Substances Act, establishing five classifications for certain drugs, substances and chemicals. The different

categories were based upon medical use as well as potential for abuse. The first schedule was reserved for drugs with a high possibility for abuse and what the DEA describes as "the potential to create severe psychological and/or physical dependence." Schedule 1 drugs were also thought to have "no currently acceptable medical use." Marijuana was temporarily placed in that category, alongside the likes of heroin, lysergic acid diethylamide (better known

as LSD) and methylene-dioxymethamphetamine (aka "meth").

Two years later, in opposition to President Richard Nixon, the National Commission on Marihuana and Drug Abuse actually recommended that marijuana be removed from that Schedule 1 designation, because it didn't pose as serious a threat as the other substances on the list. The commission's report concluded that "the absence of adequate

understanding of the effects of the drug," along with "lurid accounts of (largely unsubstantiated) 'marijuana atrocities'" committed by users, had created a false impression in the minds of the public and government officials. The report recommended decriminalizing some levels of pot possession, but Nixon rejected the findings. The Department of Justice kept pot on the Schedule 1 list—where it remains.

2

Medical Benefits

A single
marijuana plant
can yield a pound
of weed in a year.

WHAT YOU NEED TO KNOW TO TAP INTO EVERYDAY

CANNABIS HEALING

A quick-and-easy guide to help you understand plant-based relief.

Integrating cannabis into everyday life can bring happiness to the most mundane of chores, as well as relief from aches and pains. It can also bring a higher joy to an exercise regimen. But how do you go about making it part of your routine, and balance everyday situations with societal norms around an acceptable use of cannabis?

THE TRUTH
There is no one-size-fits-all approach to cannabis. While most pharmaceuticals have a single active pharmaceutical ingredient (API), cannabis is a complex plant with many active ingredients (cannabinoids and terpenes). This makes it therapeutically versatile but also presents challenges (and, by the way, so does the variety of strains and product names).

Cannabis can bring relief and joy to daily life—just do your research.

THE OTHER TRUTH

Finding the best cannabis product, dosage, consumption method and basic protocol for a particular condition often requires trial and error. Most of us have the same basic internal mechanisms and gears, and everything is placed in the same spots. However, our unique internal imprint differs, depending on our gender, age, hormonal levels, health conditions, previous cannabis and/or alcohol use, and so on. Oh, and cannabis can affect the same person differently at different stages of life.

THE FINAL TRUTH

It's important to work with a health practitioner—someone you trust—in the cannabis space, as well as your primary doctor. They may be the same person; they may not be. In any case, with the right guidance, you can tap into a whole new world of cannabis healing. We asked Pamela Hadfield, co-founder of HelloMD (an online cannabis telemedicine and product-sales company), for sound advice and where to begin. "It's a real mental shift for people to think about plant-based medicine," she says. "It's challenging, simply because the same brand, strain and ratio will work for a while and then, in six months, perhaps the crops change

> ## "IT'S A REAL MENTAL SHIFT FOR PEOPLE TO THINK ABOUT PLANT-BASED MEDICINE…. YOU HAVE TO BE FLEXIBLE."
>
> **PAMELA HADFIELD, HELLOMD**

or you change, and it all changes. You have to be flexible. Cannabis can be a lock and key for helping you with a specific condition, and it is possible to find the right solution for you. It can work wonders…but it takes patience. If you are serious about cannabis, it can take months to find the right product and dosage. It's a shame to hear someone try one thing, say it doesn't work and then give up, because it's possible that person has simply not yet found what works for them as an individual."

Whether you are struggling with a specific health issue, or life just needs a boost, cannabis can provide relief (Note: not a cure, but relief)—and here is where to begin the conversation.

BOOST YOUR IMMUNE SYSTEM

"I get this question a lot, on a daily basis," says Hadfield. "CBD can help stave off the common cold and sinus infections. The difference between one cold a season and a cold once a month has to do with CBD's anti-microbial and anti-inflammatory properties. Many studies have looked at CBD's effect on the immune system. These studies have found that CBD is an immunomodulator—it can both suppress and boost the immune system, depending on the circumstances. Currently, there is no research that explicitly shows that CBD cures the common cold or flu, but we do know it has powerful anti-inflammatory properties." Remember that you're dealing with a virus (antibiotics are for bacteria); you want to boost your immunity so your body can fight it off.

Hadfield takes a 20:1 ratio in tincture form daily. "And there's some benefit to CBD in a tincture form for tea…perhaps a turmeric tea with an extra bump of CBD. Personally, I found that after I started taking CBD daily, I no longer experienced the sinus infections that I'd had multiple times a year since I was a child. That was a game-changer for me."

INSOMNIA

In a CBD usage study, HelloMD and Brightfield Group found

that 60 percent of the 2,400 participants used CBD to treat insomnia or other sleep problems. Some found relief from vaporizers (for people who have a hard time falling asleep, but can usually stay asleep once they do). Other evidence suggests that CBD can promote wakefulness, so inhaling a small amount throughout the day keeps you awake and able to maintain a normal sleep cycle.

Hadfield takes an edible mint with 2.5mg THC an hour before bedtime to fall, and stay, asleep. Edibles can provide long-lasting sedative effects "and relieve that dreaded 2 a.m. wake-up time.

It is important to measure your marijuana use, especially when it comes to sleep. If you take too much THC, it can have the opposite effect and actually keep you awake—so you want to start low and go slow until you find the dose that puts you to sleep and keeps you asleep."

ANXIETY

Anxiety is another common condition that affects millions. It can cause restless nights. It can be a symptom of chronic pain, menopause and/or daily stress, among other things. "Anxiety is a scourge on society," says Hadfield. "There are so many factors to blame—from social media, where we never allow ourselves to be at peace, to one big event, such as public speaking. Or it can be caused by the buildup of smaller stressful moments. Anxiety has so many causes, and it can be passing or chronic,

but in either case, it affects a person's overall quality of life."

There is existing preclinical evidence that strongly supports CBD as a treatment for panic disorder, generalized anxiety disorder, social anxiety disorder, obsessive–compulsive disorder and post-traumatic stress disorder when administered acutely. CBD has a broad pharmacological profile, including interactions with several receptors known to regulate fear- and anxiety-related behaviors, and it can ease the body and mind back into a state of balance.

PAIN AND INFLAMMATION

"Chronic pain and inflammation can be the origin of many other health conditions," explains Hadfield. "Unfortunately, in society, we have seen that opiates have been the go-to for pain relief when, in fact, they were not made for long-lasting pain but for acute

pain. In a recent study we conducted with UC Berkeley, we found that 92 percent of participants strongly agreed that they preferred cannabis over opioids to treat medical conditions, and 81 percent strongly agreed that cannabis by itself was more effective than taking cannabis with opioids. The results were similar when using cannabis with non-opiate-based pain medications."

For chronic pain, a 1:1 CBD:THC ratio seems to work best for people. "For some, CBD alone helps with chronic pain," says Hadfield. "It's how the body metabolizes it. Smoking flower can provide pain relief; for others, vaping works." Comfortable with neither? Try a gel cap.

Inflammation is a common condition we all experience. There is short-term inflammation caused by fevers or sore muscles, and then there is more chronic inflammation, such as asthma or Crohn's disease. Studies now show that CBD is an effective anti-inflammatory and that it may reduce the inflammatory response within our bodies.

EXERCISE

As a longtime yogi and outdoor enthusiast, Hadfield consumes a low dose of cannabis (around 2mg) 30 minutes before start time to feel more relaxed and present.

THE CANNABIS-YOGA CONNECTION

Cannabis and yoga have been connected for thousands of years, both for religious and ceremonial purposes. It is believed that Lord Shiva, the destroyer and creator god in Hinduism—who is also the god of yoga—had an injury that was healed after consuming cannabis.

Some people believe that this religious connection is why cannabis was initially incorporated into yoga practice. In either case, yoga and cannabis seem at home with each other. Cannabis can help to deepen a yoga practice by relaxing muscles, easing anxiety and allowing the practitioner to drop into the movements more easily.

66

YOGA AND
CANNABIS
CAN EXPAND
YOUR OWN
SELF-AWARENESS
AND OPEN A
SPIRITUAL DOOR."

PAMELA HADFIELD

"I am dialed into what I am doing at the moment, but I don't go past the point of no return. It's not about getting high; it is about finding a subtherapeutic dosage—a barely perceptible sense that allows me to enter flow state. It's about optimizing an experience and being in the moment, not leaving it.

"What's most interesting about exercise and cannabis is that when we exercise, we release endocannabinoids, which bind to our cannabinoid receptors within our central nervous system," Hadfield adds. "Some believe this is one of the reasons we experience that well-known runner's high. Cannabis supplements our system with phytocannabinoids, which also bind to our receptors and seem to mimic this feeling. Perhaps this is why so many runners consume cannabis—it enhances a feeling they know very well. Studies have shown that consuming cannabis can produce a runner's high that lasts longer, since THC stored in fat is slowly diffused back in the blood via fat tissue."

The keys to cannabis-workout success: play and microdosing. With free-form activities, play joyfully; chill out; get creative; and connect with cannabis. Feed your curiosity and enjoy the transformative nature of both yoga and cannabis.

CBD MAY HELP

1

EASE SINUS PRESSURE AND HEADACHES (VAPE)

2

SOOTHE ACHES AND PAINS (SALVE OR FULL-BODY SOAK IN THE TUB)

3

REDUCE NAUSEA (TEA, TINCTURE)

4

CALM A COUGH (TEA AND HONEY)

HEALTH ENLIGHTENMENT

How cannabis may help stomp out pain, ease anxiety, relieve PMS symptoms, make your skin glow, and more...much more.

Doctors are increasingly recommending cannabis to treat a variety of health conditions.

T wo years ago, Marisa Zeppieri reached her breaking point. Since being diagnosed with lupus, an autoimmune disorder, she'd tried just about every prescription pain reliever out there to cope with joint and muscle pain. After a series of allergic reactions, she'd decided to stick with over-the-counter Tylenol, but she was taking more and more and not getting relief. At a friend's urging, she finally gave cannabis a try. "Within 10 minutes, the pain was gone," says Zeppieri. "I couldn't believe it."

Zeppieri, now 40, says she wishes she had turned to the plant sooner. What held her back, she admits, was fear—and a lack of knowledge. "I grew up in a community where [marijuana] was 'bad,'" she says. "I didn't understand that it's the CBD that helps most with chronic pain, and that's not what gets you high."

Cannabidiol, or CBD for short, is the main chemical compound in weed believed to be responsible for a slew of health benefits. The other main "active ingredient" is THC (tetrahydrocannabinol), a psychoactive compound that makes users feel high. You'll find CBD in both marijuana and hemp, which are different varieties of the cannabis plant, but hemp usually contains only trace amounts of THC.

CBD-only products that are derived from hemp and contain less than 0.3% THC (the federal threshold) are more widely available throughout the U.S. Many of these products are also designed to promote dewier skin (like the CannaSmack Luxe line) or smooth out wrinkles (like Cannabliss Organics Age Defying Lotion).

It's not just hype, says Joshua Zeichner, MD, director of cosmetic and clinical research in dermatology at Mount Sinai Hospital in New York City. "CBD binds to receptors in the skin and has soothing properties. The oil itself is rich in fatty acids and emollient ingredients that hydrate and soothe the skin."

There are also a number of CBD-only products, like Sagely Natural Relief & Recovery Cream, that are aimed at easing run-of-the-mill aches. Hemp-derived products are legal throughout the country, and some people find that CBD alone is enough to ease their discomfort, whether they're plagued by arthritis, migraines or sore muscles. But for more severe pain, you might need to add some THC in the mix.

"It's very patient-specific, but a blend of THC and CBD tends to be most effective," says Laura Borgelt, PharmD, a professor at the University of Colorado Skaggs School of Pharmacy and Pharmaceutical Sciences. She says that there's a synergistic effect between the two compounds, and, in some cases, a relatively small amount of THC is all that's needed.

Skin-care products containing CBD are one of the fastest-growing segments of the CBD market.

YOU DON'T HAVE TO GET HIGH

Aliza Sherman lives in Alaska, where marijuana is legal for recreational as well as medical use. She says she doesn't frown on people who use the drug recreationally, but that she herself had no interest in doing so when she started researching cannabis in early 2016.

"I had arthritis in my neck, and I had tried all sort of things and nothing was working," Sherman says. Her initial intrigue eventually led her to found Ellementa, an online and in-person network for women who are interested in cannabis for health and wellness. The more she learned, the more she realized that everything she thought she knew about the drug was wrong.

"I was so afraid it was going to mess up my brain," recalls Sherman, who says she discovered that the reason cannabis was historically prohibited was mostly political: "It is not a dangerous 'gateway' drug." In fact, some physicians are now using marijuana to help their patients wean off opioids.

Today, Sherman is an occasional user; cannabis eases her neck pain and helps her sleep when her mind is racing. She enjoys visiting new marijuana shops to explore their offerings—in Alaska, it's similar to walking

> ## CANNABIS IS GAINING TRACTION AMONG HEALTH PROFESSIONALS."
>
> **ALIZA SHERMAN, FOUNDER OF ELLEMENTA**

into a liquor store—but she admits that some retailers do a better job of catering to mature women than others. "I walked into this beautiful store the other day, and the guy behind the counter said, 'You can get really messed up with this.' And I was thinking, 'Come on. I'm 53; I have silver hair. That's not what I'm looking for.'"

If that's not what you're looking for, either, you'll want to pay close attention to the CBD-to-THC ratio. Not only is CBD packed with medicinal properties, but it also tempers the psychoactive effects of THC, says Borgelt. Assuming you live in a state where medical marijuana is legal, ask your doctor to make some initial suggestions. "If a strain is CBD-rich, the CBD-to-THC ratio might be 20:1 or 50:1," she says.

Your dose matters too, and it turns out that less is often more effective for a variety of symptoms, says Dustin Sulak, DO, an integrative medicine physician in Maine and founder of healer.com, a site focused on educating patients about medical marijuana. He's a fan of microdosing, which he defines as "using a dose of THC that is below the threshold of impairment and other unwanted psychoactive effects. For most people, this is less than 5mg [THC]."

Smoking is still a popular way to ingest cannabis, but many find tinctures and oils to be more convenient (and discreet).

65

ONE DRUG, MANY BENEFITS

To understand why a smaller amount of cannabis usually works better, you need to know a little about how the drug works in general. It boils down to the endocannabinoid system. In the 1990s, scientists discovered this body system, which runs from head to toe and sometimes overlaps with the central nervous system, Borgelt explains. "A lot of times, people overstimulate the receptors, which can have adverse effects," she says.

The presence of cannabinoid receptors all over your body explains why cannabis may be useful for a wide array of ailments. The other part of the puzzle: Cannabis isn't really one drug; the plant is packed with "hundreds of different compounds," says Sherman.

As more about cannabis is being uncovered by scientists, it's gaining traction among health-care professionals. In June 2018, the FDA approved Epidiolex to treat seizures. And although there's no THC in it, it's poised to become the first cannabis-derived prescription medication in the U.S.

Aside from seizures, the best-proven uses for cannabis are for chronic pain, chemo-associated nausea and muscle spasms related to multiple sclerosis, according to the National Academies of Sciences, Engineering and Medicine. There's also some solid research to support its use for sleep problems, especially in people with pain disorders or neurological ailments.

Other small studies—and anecdotal reports—suggest that cannabis might help with everything from severe menstrual cramps and sexual dysfunction to migraines and anxiety. Choosing the right strain is important: One might increase appetite, whereas another could actually suppress it, notes Sherman. "It's not a cure-all, and it's not 'one plant fits all.' It's more like different versions of this plant can fit some things," she says.

> " [CANNABIS HAS] VERY FEW SIDE EFFECTS AND ALMOST NO INTERACTIONS WITH OTHER DRUGS."
>
> **MATTHEW MINTZ, MD**

If you have a medical-marijuana card, you can walk into a dispensary and ask for recommendations based on what has worked well for others with similar conditions. Another important benefit of buying from a legal dispensary is that it's regulated, so you can find out how much CBD and THC a product contains as well as get some info about its terpene (aromatic oil) profile.

SHOULD YOU TRY IT?

Many health experts, including Borgelt, believe that cannabis should be considered a last resort —at least until more research has been completed and better regulations are in place. "I don't think we're at the point where it's a first- or even second-line treatment," she says. "But when other FDA-approved treatments aren't working, there may be times when cannabis can help."

Matthew Mintz, MD, a board-certified internist in Maryland who started prescribing medical marijuana soon after it became medically legal in his state in 2017, says he's beginning to believe some patients might benefit from turning to cannabis sooner. "Prescription sleep medications work, but they interact with a lot of other medicines and there are lots of side effects," he notes. "NSAIDs, including ibuprofen, can

Tinctures can be taken sublingually and take effect more quickly than other edibles.

> **"It's very patient-specific, but a blend of THC and CBD tends to be most effective."**
>
> **LAURA BORGELT, PHARMD**

mess with your kidneys and cause stomach problems. Cannabis doesn't do any of that. There are very few side effects and almost no interactions with other drugs."

That said, interactions are not impossible, especially when it comes to THC. It's best to discuss your needs with a doctor, who should also be able to weigh in on delivery methods.

Cannabis is available in many different forms, from topical salves, patches and suppositories to edibles, tinctures, vape pens and joints. If your goal is to get healthier—not just high— steer clear of joints. For those who like to inhale, vaping is a better option. "The combustion is a problem. The carbon gets in your lungs and destroys them," says Mintz.

Borgelt prefers liquid tinctures, which you swallow or put under your tongue. "With a tincture, you're getting a known dose, and it's easier to adjust. With vaping, it depends on how deep you're inhaling, how long you hold your breath, etc."

If medical marijuana is legal in your state but you're having trouble finding an expert to guide you, Zeppieri suggests heading to HelloMD, a website she had used to connect with a physician who reviewed her medical records and discussed her symptoms before writing a prescription.

Zeppieri knows that some people still question whether cannabis is a legitimate medication. She gets it—she used to be among the skeptics —but she now says that anyone who's in pain should give it a try. "I've spoken to hundreds of [lupus] patients," says Zeppieri, who founded the website LupusChick. "Everyone who's tried it has been able to lower their dose of prescription pain medication or get off it completely."

OUR EXPERTS

MATTHEW MINTZ, MD
Located in Bethesda, Maryland, Mintz is a certifying provider by Maryland Medical Cannabis Commission (MMCC) and one of the few physicians in the state who can issue a letter of recommendation for qualifying patients to receive medical marijuana in Maryland.

LAURA BORGELT, PHARMD
An associate professor at the University of Colorado Anschutz Medical Campus, Borgelt focuses on women's health. Her initial interest in medical marijuana started when she was asked clinical questions about its use by pregnant and lactating women.

EVALUATING THE MOST EFFECTIVE MEDICAL-MARIJUANA STRAINS

Four growers offer their thoughts on types of medicinal cannabis.

ACDC

"Also commonly called Charlotte's Web, this classic CBD-dominant variety rose to fame due to its reported effectiveness in controlling seizures associated with epilepsy. While ACDC can be a difficult plant to cultivate, its flower is consistently pleasant, with notes of sweet grass and light citrus." —*Walker*

Chem 4

"A high-THC strain, this has had great success treating pain. Chem 4 is also high in the plant compound beta-myrcene. This combination tends to help patients with a lot of pain. Chem 4 tests for THC in the high 20 percent range and packs a punch with its terpene profile. Most use it at night for pain control before bed." —*Peters*

Blue Dragon Desert Frost

"It's a flower born of a single coveted miracle seed that was gifted to us by a patient who swore that it was the best for her anxiety and pain and wanted a steady supply. We got lucky that it was female and an amazing rare strain. She tests at around 15–18 percent CBD and 1 percent THC, so one might not initially believe her strong CBD dominance by smell alone. Trichomes-laden purple buds bring a subtle euphoria and relief." —*Rivero*

Corazon

"Rich in CBD, Corazon has a way of earning a soft spot in your heart. We have been donating this particular strain to a young patient with severe epilepsy, and it seems to be the only one that works for him. He has gone from many seizures every day to nearly zero, allowing him to ride his bike again and enjoy life. With a 20:1 ratio of CBD to THC, it's no wonder this strain works wonders—but there is definitely a bit of magic involved as well." —*Rivero*

THE EXPERTS

Dan Sloat
Founder of the Colorado farm Alpinstash

Mason Walker
CEO of Oregon's East Fork Cultivars

Jesse Peters
Owner of the Oregon-based Eco Firma Farms

Laura Day Rivero
Operations Manager for Yerba Buena Farms, in Oregon

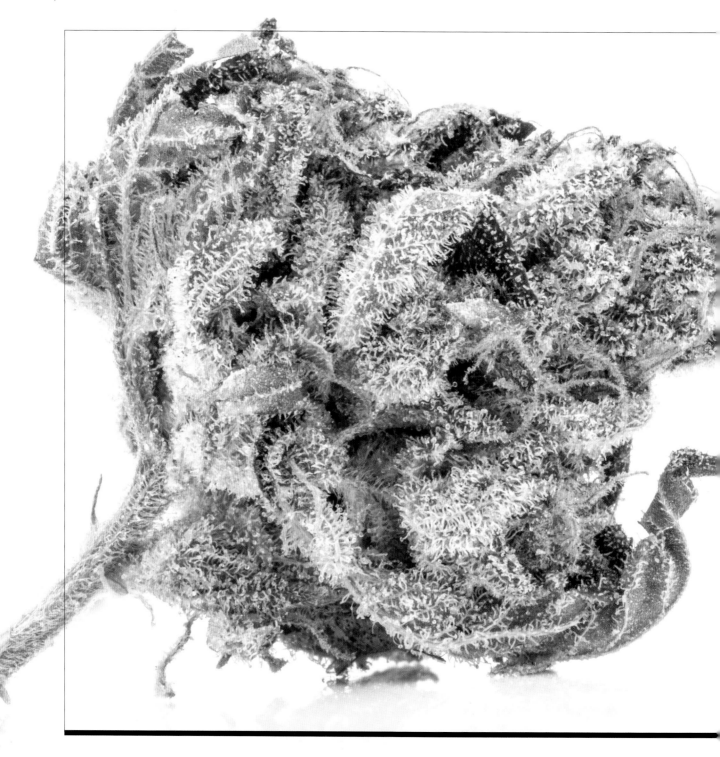

Dosido

"This strain packs a powerful psychoactive punch, with an immediate calming body stone, coupled with a heavy mental space that is deeply relaxing and offers instant pain relief to many. One of our most beautiful and trichomes-caked cultivars, this one boasts a rare non-myrcene-dominant terpene profile with nerolidol and limonene." —*Rivero*

LSD

LSD (not to be confused with the drug best known for its psychological effects) is a high-THC strain that has had success stopping seizures when converted to RSO (Rick Simpson Oil). To date, we have not been able to nail down what part of the profile is so unique, but it seems to work. The genotype we have is exceptionally difficult to grow, but, in the end, we keep her around specifically for her medicinal purposes." —*Peters*

Maui Bubble Gift

"This has a 2:1 ratio, CBD to THC. MBG is one of our most popular medicinal strains. It's a rare variety that's easy to have issues with, but if treated well, it grows strong. We have many patients who have treated a host of issues with great success. Her cannabinoid and terpene profile seems to treat people very well. Patients have used it for Parkinson's disease, cerebral palsy and cancer." —*Peters*

Lemmiwinks

"With its potent, sweet grape-flavored buds, Lemmiwinks is one of our top strains for relaxation and sleep. It's one of my personal go-tos to help with the muscle spasms and pain I have due to nerve issues. The calming effect is perfect after a hard day at work; it's a great nighttime smoke." —*Sloat*

Pineapple Jager
"We bred this variety by combining a southern Oregon favorite strain called Jager (aka Purple Hindu Kush) with Pineapple Tsu. The result is a 3:1 CBD-to-THC plant, packed with a diverse range of terpenes. The high terpene content rounds out the cannabinoids for a potent yet comfortable array of effects. A considerable nose stands out in this variety, with notes of tropical fruit and 'fuel' coming through the strongest." —Walker

Ringo's Gift
"It's a legendary CBD powerhouse named after the late Lawrence Ringo, a pioneer in CBD-rich cannabis breeding and development. (A California native, he started growing cannabis at age 15 for back pain.) Ringo's Gift has been noted for its alleged association with clear-headed pain relief. This variety produces a dense flower with a peppery nose." —Walker

Snoop's Dream
"This is good for the 'introduction to cannabis' smoker, who wants to dip a toe in the water. Cannabis is not the answer for everyone, but this is a great strain to start with—especially for those who are wary of the anxiety or paranoia sometimes associated with cannabis use. A cross of Master Kush and Blue Dream, the terpene profile is good for anxiety, PTSD or panic attacks." —Peters

Platinum Tiger Cookies
"A high-THC/sativa hybrid for relaxation, both physical and mental. The sativa influences of this strain can cause the giggles, which makes it perfect for social settings or enjoying a private moment. The touch of indica takes away any edge or paranoia-inducing aspects. Has a unique cheesy, lemony, funk flavor." —Sloat

Sister Wife
"This has a 20:1 CBD-to-THC ratio. It smells like blueberries and has a unique pinecone look. The high amount of CBD is great for inflammation and pain disorders, while the low THC (0.05 percent or less) helps relax the muscles and mind. It's also particularly good for menstrual cramps." —Sloat

Strawberry Satori
"This variety shows high levels of linalool, a terpene that is commonly found in lavender. Early evidence suggests it may be effective against anxiety and stress, particularly in PTSD. Traditionally a THC-dominant variety, we're working to breed a CBD-rich variety that maintains the linalool profile. Characterized by its large flower structure, Strawberry Satori has a savory fruit nose, backed by notes of leather." —Walker

Smoking marijuana after chemo changed Brianne's life.

COMFORT
AFTER CHEMO

A breast cancer survivor
finds help and hope with cannabis.

May 9, 2012, is seared in my memory. That's the day I was diagnosed with a very aggressive collection of tumors in my chest. I was in the shower and I felt a lump in my armpit. I knew that something wasn't right and went to see my gynecologist right after work (I was an embroiderer at a small factory in Brick Township, New Jersey). He found another tumor in my breast. Mammograms and ultrasounds found two more. On May 22, before removing the tumors, I began a very aggressive chemotherapy protocol for five months, to bomb my entire body to destroy any growth and eliminate any possibility of stage 4, which is terminal.

When I had to go through all that chemotherapy while having to work and raise two children, my immediate thought was, Let's load up on the weed. I had smoked before I got sick and saw how cannabis had helped a few friends who were dealing with cancer. The difference now is that I don't really get high, I just feel better. It allows me to feel normal. It became a whole new thing for me after cancer. I don't remember what it was like before, when it was fun. Now it's a necessity.

Chemo made me feel like a toxic bomb went off in my body—and when you're trying to deal with the side effects and the whole stress of having cancer, marijuana just takes away everything. I would use it to eat, to sleep, to feel like I could get out of bed and move, but the main thing was the nausea. I was working nine-hour days, so when I got home, I was absolutely taxed. My bones hurt, and cannabis was the only thing that worked. It makes you step out of your head first, then it relieves your symptoms. It's hard to describe— but you definitely leave your body.

After all the chemo, on November 9, I had a bilateral mastectomy and a lymph-node dissection with reconstruction. I then had to undergo 25 days of radiation to make sure all the

> ## "[MEDICAL MARIJUANA] MAKES YOU STEP OUT OF YOUR HEAD FIRST, THEN IT RELIEVES YOUR SYMPTOMS. IT'S HARD TO DESCRIBE—BUT YOU DEFINITELY LEAVE YOUR BODY."
> **BRIANNE DIOMEDE**

cancer was eradicated. It was like, burn the forest down. But the radiation caused so much damage, I had to have five fat-grafting surgeries over the next three years on top of working and trying to be a good mom to my kids, who are now 15 and 7. They're my whole world, so it was quite a shock when I got into a little bit of trouble with Child Protective Services in 2014.

"I'M LIKE A DIFFERENT PERSON"
I had signed up for psychotherapy through the state, because I didn't have any health insurance and had to get drug-tested because it's a state program. When I came up positive for marijuana, they had to call CPS. They felt really bad, but they had to do it for legal reasons. My doctor had to write that it was necessary for my treatment because I couldn't really take anything else. CPS is not fun. That was the last thing I needed in my condition.

Needless to say, it was a huge relief when I was finally able to get a medical-marijuana card last June. I have refused all pharmaceuticals because of the side effects, with the exception of pain meds postsurgeries. When the program was first started in 2010, you had to have a terminal illness, ALS or AIDS, but now it covers PTSD and people with

Marijuana has allowed Brianne to enjoy life with her family.

musculoskeletal spasticity, like myself, who were damaged by radiation. I can get the best-quality flower at my dispensary, with all terpenes listed, and CBG/CBD/THC levels to help me find the best strains to get through my day and night, since I live in constant pain.

I have two broken ribs that refuse to heal, but I also have to keep a house going, so cannabis has been my lifesaver for it all. I use it to sleep, eat, create art (for extra income, since I'm on disability), function, uplift and balance out the stress and anxiety of being limited.

I get 1 ounce a month, which costs about $300 to $400, but I get a 20 percent discount because I'm on Social Security. It's not cheap, but it's really, really good. Knowing that it's not been sprayed with anything and with the different levels of terpenes, I know what I'm getting. Two of the strains I like are Montana Silvertip, a hybrid for the daytime, and Lavender, an indica for the nighttime. Silvertip is very high in a cannabinoid called CBG, which has been shown to promote bone growth. My ribs don't hurt when I use it.

I smoke about half-a-dozen bowls during the day and about half that at night. It makes me feel like a human being. My husband will tell you—when it runs out, I'm a different person. It's like not having coffee in the morning. My youngest is too young to know what it is. My oldest is aware of it, but I don't do it in front of her. She understands that it is a medicine. She knows kids in her class who use it, but she realizes there's a medicinal aspect to it. There's no judgment from her.

Marijuana is not addictive, but feeling happy is addictive, feeling relaxed is addictive. I don't see myself ever stopping using it, because I've been hacked apart so many times, there's no going back to normal. I just want it to be legal for everybody who needs it, regardless of income or status, and available at a reasonable price.

—*Brianne Diomede*

THE STUDY OF
WOMEN
AND WEED

The effects of cannabinoids have been well-studied in men, but recent data indicates they may not affect women in the same way. Inherent differences in sensitivity may explain our response to psychoactive drugs.

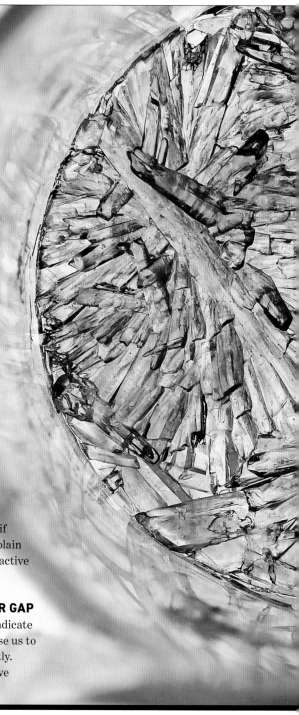

T he first thing you should know about Rebecca Craft, PhD, a professor in the department of psychology at Washington State University (WSU), is that she spends most of her days studying how male and female rats get high. While the biology of rats and humans is similar, it's not exactly one-to-one. But until recently, most drug research, in general, has been conducted mainly on males—animal or human. Craft's goal: to determine if gender differences can explain how we respond to psychoactive drugs like cannabinoids.

FILLING IN THE GENDER GAP

Some of Craft's findings indicate that biology may predispose us to experience drugs differently. Take THC, the psychoactive

Research behind
sensitivity to
cannabis compounds
has just begun.

compound in marijuana: Research shows it has a more potent analgesic and sedative effects in females, who metabolize it differently than males.

Other studies have revealed the complex relationship between THC and CBD (cannabidiol, the nonpsychoactive compound in marijuana) and how their interactions may affect conditions like pain and inflammation. Since women tend to suffer more from inflammatory pain conditions like rheumatoid arthritis, more research needs to be done, says Craft.

Her studies have shown that while there was not a significant effect on pain reduction when CBD and THC were taken together, higher doses (two times a day for five days) did create an interaction, with CBD decreasing THC's effects. It's this kind of research that can help indicate if the medical community needs to adjust the way women and men use cannabis to treat pain and inflammation, notes Craft.

DIGGING DEEPER

Carrie Cuttler, PhD, a clinical assistant professor of psychology at WSU, also researches the interaction of THC and CBD. One of her most recent studies looked to explain perceived changes in symptoms of depression, anxiety

and stress as a function of both THC and CBD. The result: Medical-cannabis users reported a 50 percent overall reduction in depression and a 58 percent drop in anxiety and stress. Just two puffs of cannabis were enough to reduce ratings of depression and anxiety. Cannabis that had the highest levels of CBD but was low in THC was associated with the

largest changes in depression ratings; cannabis high in both CBD and THC had the greatest perceived change on stress level.

But the study also found that while both women and men experienced these changes, women reported a significantly greater decrease in anxiety following cannabis consumption compared to men. (It also found

insomnia and vivid dreams as withdrawal symptoms; women are more likely to report nausea and anxiety. Finally, men are more likely than women to report "the munchies" and an altered sense of time as acute effects of cannabis, while women are more likely than men to report a loss of appetite during acute cannabis intoxication, notes Cuttler.

COMBINING FORCES

Craft and Cuttler aren't the only ones exploring how cannabis may affect men and women differently. Research on the differences between sex hormones, cannabinoid receptors, muscle mass and fat-tissue distribution and other important factors continue to draw attention.

The trick is to find a way to share research information among professionals and the public. The recently formed Institute for Cannabis Research (ICR) in Pueblo, Colorado, may help. The multidisciplinary research center was created in 2016 to provide education, research and service, including hosting an annual conference where scientists, health-care professionals, marijuana advocates and activists can gather to share information—and learn just how much gender plays a part in our feelings about marijuana.

that long-term use was associated with increased symptoms of depression among both genders.)

Prior research has pointed out other gender differences. Women are more likely than men to report using cannabis to treat irritable bowel syndrome (IBS), anxiety, nausea, anorexia and headaches/migraines. Men are more likely than women to report

BIOLOGY MAY PREDISPOSE PEOPLE TO EXPERIENCE DRUGS DIFFERENTLY.

ALTERNATIVE MEDICINE FOR YOUR SKIN

An injury sparked holistic dermatologist Jeanette Jacknin's interest in CBD for the skin.

Jeanette Jacknin defined integrative dermatology and discussed holistic treatments in her 2001 book *Smart Medicine for Your Skin*. And the board-certified dermatologist's belief in combining conventional dermatology with holistic options has gained traction over the years. This includes treating the whole person, taking into account psychological and social factors, rather than just physical symptoms. So in 2016, when Jacknin tore cartilage in her ankle and a friend suggested CBD instead of pharmaceuticals, it was her medical background and understanding of the limits of health care that led her to study the skin science behind cannabinoids.

"Hemp oil has great benefits," says Jacknin. "Even with small amounts of CBD, it is rich in omega-3 fatty acids and vitamins. Hemp molecules are small and penetrate the skin well, and have moisturizing and nutritional properties."

So how does it work? The skin has its own endocannabinoid system that regulates hormone and protein production, including cytokines, which are involved in the immune response, and cannabinoid lipids, which regulate homeostasis and skin inflammation. Human tissues have at least two types of cannabinoid receptors. CB1 receptors mediate the inhibition of neurotransmitter release (involved with euphoria in the

The future of cannabis and skin care looks bright... and glowing.

brain, but also in the skin), while CB2s modulate cytokine release (usually involved with the anti-inflammatory effect). A receptor can recognize and bind with molecules, including interactions with phytocannabinoids from cannabis (CBD and THC).

The good news: The binding affinity of particular cannabinoids to certain types of receptors within the endocannabinoid system have implications for epidermal differentiation (acne, inflammation) as well as skin development (aging and new cell growth).

**AS CBD SKIN-CARE
LINES AND SPA THERAPIES
POP UP EVERYWHERE,
HERE ARE
DR. JACKNIN'S
RECOMMENDATIONS**

Read the Ingredients List

A long list of unpronounceable names is a red flag. If hemp or CBD oil is at the end, it probably contains very little. Check the milligram number.

Always Patch-Test

Test a small amount on the back of your hand for a few hours.

Check for Essential Oils

These are sometimes mixed into a product; if you have sensitive skin, try unscented.

Look for Massage Oils and Deeper Pain-Relief Products

CBD oils are a great start, but a transdermal product (like a patch) can get under the skin and straight to the muscle. Beware: Cheap products often use ineffective adhesive.

THE FITNESS BOOST

For many women today, cannabis is an essential part of their pre- and post-workout plan.

For Los Angeles artist Brynn Gelbard, who owns a custom art-design studio with her wife, getting high and working out coexisted separately in her life until a friend invited her to a dance class.

"I've always been more of a tomboy," says Gelbard. "So when I went to class, I was so self-conscious. But when I smoked, it was like I could fly." Gelbard found that not only did her self-doubt melt away, but she was more focused on the movement. "I could escape my body issues and just focus on the beat, all while being totally relaxed."

It's a sentiment echoed time and time again by women who are looking to maximize their fitness by reaching a heightened state of calm and focus. "As an athlete," explains Gelbard. "It puts me in my body. It puts me in my mind. It helps me to be present."

However, while it may make women feel like they can really zone in or out of a workout, there is an added benefit: pain relief.

Brandon Anthony, creator of CannabisMOVEMENT in Los Angeles, a class he defines as a "guided moving musical meditation," shares an experience that led him to create a new kind of weed-based workout. A former dancer and choreographer, Anthony became a seasoned fitness expert who trained women at SoulCycle, Equinox, Yoga Works and Flywheel Sports. His first "aha" high moment happened a few years ago before a challenging run/hike.

"I decided to have a little weed before going to run, thinking 'I'll just enjoy the day,'" he says. "Then I get up there and had the most badass run. My breath felt so expansive. My lungs felt open. I felt energized." And there was no soreness.

Soon, Anthony was using the plant in a range of workouts, including weightlifting, yoga, swimming and dance. "There was an immediate improvement to my form, my focus, my connection to the physical movement," he says. He wanted to share it with his students, but worried about what his clients would think. (At the time, cannabis was legal only for medical patients.) "I didn't want to offend or lose students or have them make assumptions," shares Anthony.

> ## 66
> LOW-DOSE IS
> BEST FOR YOGA.
> IT'S A CREAMY,
> GOOEY
> BODY HIGH."
>
> YOGA TEACHER
> DEE DUSSAULT

He likens the next period to a time when he had to hide his being gay. "It was like being in the closet again—the cannabis closet," Anthony says. Once cannabis was legal in California, Anthony shared his experience with students and created his popular dance class, which women flock to. Anthony favors sativa varieties for women who are new to cannabis. "It's more social and energetic," he says. "Dosage is key, too. I like to use a low-dose, edible powder. It gets you to a place where you feel energized and awake."

TURNING OVER A NEW LEAF

Jessica, a 37-year-old teacher and mom, first integrated indica edibles during one of Anthony's dance workshops. "Free-form dance is spiritual and cathartic," says Jessica. "The con of it is that I'm in my head, wrestling with personal conflicts. Cannabis allows me to separate myself from internal chatter." And feel good.

Jessica, like many others, takes advantage of another of the plant's compounds, cannabidiol, aka CBD—the nonpsychoactive element that can be extracted from marijuana or hemp plants and has anti-inflammatory properties. "My left shoulder has been giving me problems for 20 years," says Jessica. "I've used CBD oil to treat it, and it's really helped."

> ## 66
> ## IT HELPS YOU TO REALLY SLOW DOWN AND BE PRESENT."
> **DEE DUSSAULT**

Fran G., a creative VP in New York City, says CBD has helped her find relief and sleep better. "I used to think sore muscles meant I'd worked out hard, and I'd often have restlessness when trying to fall asleep," she says. "I used CBD lotion to soothe the soreness in my legs, particularly my calves."

While Fran admits it's not a magic pill, the cumulative effects are real. "You start to relax over time, and the discomfort pretty much dissipates." Her new bedtime ritual is a mix of CBD lotion, a few hits of a CBD pen and a cup of tea. "It puts me to sleep and lets me sleep through the night. I wake up feeling super refreshed."

Like others, Fran has found CBD benefits for both body and mind. "I use a vape pen with a cup of coffee in the morning. It helps me start

the day a bit more calm," she attests. "And I love it before a hot yoga class—I get super focused, and it makes the whole experience much more enjoyable."

Beth Bishop is owner and head coach at The Phoenix Effect, an LA fitness studio. Bishop takes a holistic approach when creating a wellness profile for new clients that includes cannabis products. "When we get an athlete in, we coach on fitness, nutrition and stress management," says Bishop.

Many regulars in her gym have found success with CBD creams and muscle rubs after they feel the burn. "The vast majority are thrilled, and few use anti-inflammatory medicines," says Bishop. She soon plans to carry a range of CBD products to fit her clients' needs. "I've always been a proponent of natural medicine," she notes. "I'll try just about anything before going pharmaceutical."

Dee Dussault, the first yoga teacher to publicly offer cannabis-enhanced yoga, teaches to thousands of women of all levels looking for something extra in their practice via her Ganja Yoga. "It helps you to really slow down and be present," says Dussault. "In yoga, you become more aware of your breath and your body." Women in her classes find vape pens, edibles or a passed joint can help maximize their self-care time. "The whole is greater than the sum of its parts," she says. "Yoga helps you relax. Cannabis helps you relax. And when you combine the two, you get a holistic effect."

Dussault suggests people experiment with what they are curious about, but she often uses relaxing, low-dose indica or hybrid strains. "Low-dose is best for yoga. It's a creamy, gooey body high."

Many of Dussault's yogis feel a significant shift, even when they opt for 100 percent CBD. "While you do not reach an altered state," she says, "you can often feel a natural high from feeling so good."

A LINGERING STIGMA

For many who are taking a toke before hitting the gym or yoga studio, there's still the fear of shame and judgment in fitness.

For Mindy, it's an occupational hazard. "I'm a teacher, so everything I do, even on my free time, is under scrutiny," she says. "The word cannabis continues to raise a red flag, unfortunately."

"I think there's a stigma in general, even for pure CBD," says Fran. "But it is a totally different feeling from weed. I love a good toke now and then, but that's for different reasons!"

Gelbard thinks shaming cannabis use often feels like part of a larger suppression. "In terms of stigmas, there's really a lot that exists around women claiming

their power in general, not just with respect to smoking pot," she says.

So will it ever change? Pros like Anthony, Dussault and Bishop want to widen the door with openness, awareness and education. "The more people in our industry who come out, the more it helps," says Anthony, who notes most people imagine a lazy stoner. "I would say 50 percent of the trainers I know use cannabis when they teach or train," he says. "People look to us for solutions. And it's another way."

Dussault says that the more women that come out of "the green closet," the more accepting everyone will be of it (and each other). Bishop sums it up in a personal way. "There's still a lot of misinformation out there," she says. "My parents don't know I use cannabis products—but would be fine with me drinking wine every night, which is so toxic and harmful. The first step is to have a good dialogue around it."

Yoga and cannabis help you relax. Together, they equal pain relief.

A CBD massage can be the key to relaxation and focus.

THE HOLY GRAIL OF CBD TREATMENTS

Taking massages to the next level.

s a woman living with multiple sclerosis (an auto-immune condition in which a body's immune cells attack the nervous system), I am always looking for ways to supplement traditional Western medicines to get my errant immune cells to stop wreaking havoc on my body. I've been on a personal search for naturally effective alternative therapies for quite some time (15 years to be exact). In the process, I've gotten very interested in the rise of cannabinoids—CBD, in particular.

Studies have been popping up all over the place, confirming that cannabinoids have a therapeutic effect, both on the symptoms and the underlying neurological damage caused by MS. While my symptoms are relatively mild (numbness and tingling in my hands and feet, low energy levels and a general brain fog that comes and goes)—nothing severe enough for hospitalization or steroids— they're enough to put a damper on my everyday life. And so I dove into the fray, medical evidence in hand, to search for ways in which cannabis extracts might help convince my immune system to stop attacking my nerves.

SELF-RESEARCH

When I first started looking into it, the cannabis-extract scene was very under-the-radar. Today it seems like you can't turn a corner without running into a CBD latte or a CBD-infused macaroon or a CBD moisturizer. I've tried them all, with varying levels of success; but when I noticed the CBD-massage "Wellness Experience" option at the Onda Beauty spa in Sag Harbor, New York, I couldn't get there fast enough. And for good reason: This massage was like the holy grail of CBD treatments. It lasted 60 minutes and featured a full-spectrum, 2100mg organic CBD oil (locally produced by a farmer right down the road), which was first worked into my back to maximize absorption and then used

CBD...HELPS ALL THE BODY'S SYSTEMS WORK IN HARMONY."

DEBRA TOWNES, MASSAGE THERAPIST

in combination with other essential oils and salves, depending on the particular needs of each area.

WHAT HAPPENED?

When I emerged, I felt like I had been bathed in fairy dust. My back and shoulders were free of knots, my hands were less tingly and I was energized and ready to go.

Debra Townes, my therapist, describes our overtaxed bodies as an orchestra, with all the instruments frenetically playing their own tune, out of sync with everyone else. "CBD comes in like a conductor, taps on the stand, and gets everyone to listen and to make music as a unified whole," she explains. "It's not a drug that forces things to be done a certain way. It's a supplement that helps all the systems work in harmony, so we can really address the issues in the tissues. It allows me to go deep, without worrying about causing the muscles too much distress."

Less friction, less stress. Less stress, more energy and clarity. More energy and clarity, better... everything.

Just think of what the world would be like if we were all operating at this level all the time.
—*Brooke Williams*

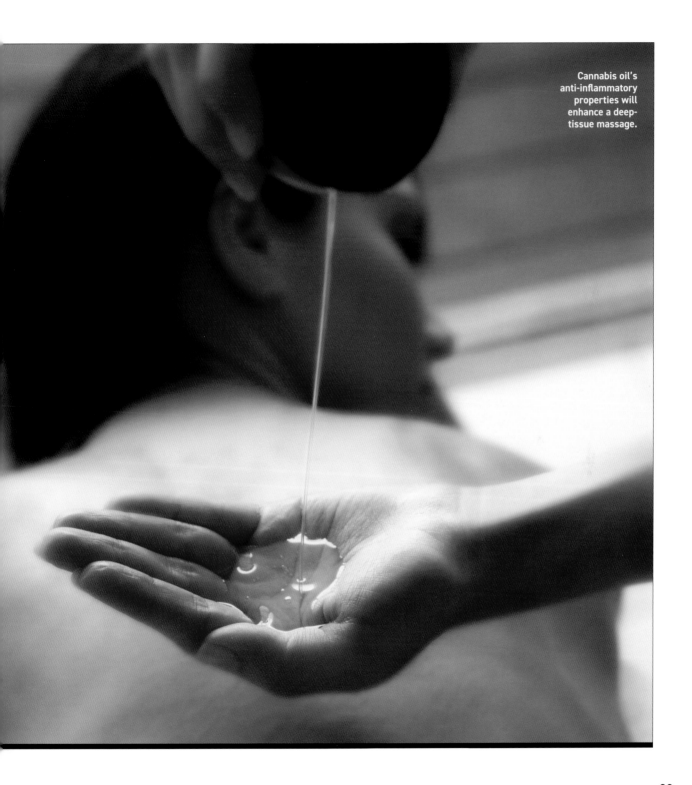

Cannabis oil's anti-inflammatory properties will enhance a deep-tissue massage.

GETTING CARDED

Everything you always needed to know about getting
your first medical-marijuana card—but were afraid to ask.

Medical Cannabis Patient Identification Card

Date of Expiration:
2013-03-21

Brittany A. Freitas
Petaluma CA 94952
ISSUED: 2012-03-22

To verify patient status visit:
https://verify.rxcbc.org

Member # 561555

As of 2016, California has issued more than 85,000 medical cards.

M

edical marijuana is now legal in 33 states and Washington D.C., but in order to obtain cannabis for your health, you'll need a medical card granting you access. So how do you go about obtaining one? We spoke with an expert, Rob Tankson, founder and CEO of prestodoctor.com, in order to learn more. Tankson's organization provides online cannabis evaluations from doctors, as well as treatment plans for patients in California, Nevada and New York.

How do you go about getting a medical marijuana card?

You first need to be evaluated by a physician. Some people go to their primary doctor, but most see a doctor who specializes in medical-cannabis evaluations because a dispensary must verify the recommendation—which can take longer with a typical doctor than with a specialist who already has an automated system in place. An online evaluation is easiest, but you can Google for medical marijuana evaluations near you, or search leafly.com's doctor locator.

FOR MEDICAL USE ONLY
as per CA Health & Safety Code sections 11362.5 and 11362.7

Purchasing hemp-based CBD doesn't require a medical card.

What does it cost?

It varies. Some evaluations are as low as $40, while others cost up to $150. We charge $70 in California and $50 for returning patients.

In California, the doctor gives you the necessary paperwork to enter a dispensary, but in most every other state, the state issues you a card or paperwork, usually in a matter of minutes or hours. Most states do charge a registration fee, from $1 in Washington State to $200 in Oregon.

What are qualifying conditions?

In some states, you have to have a terminal illness, but in many states, chronic pain or PTSD will qualify you; even anxiety qualifies in California.

Does insurance cover any of it?

Not currently, but a card is typically good for one year.

How do I go about finding a dispensary?

Just go online and Google for medical marijuana dispensaries in your state. They're even rated, just like most other types of businesses that you search.

How do you know what strain to use, and how much?

Almost 50 percent of the patients we see are new to cannabis, and it can be daunting—there are so many questions. We give every patient a personalized treatment plan that says, "You have this condition; this is what the doctor recommends, and you should consume it this way [by vaping, as edibles or in tinctures]. You should do it this often and at this time of day." We typically recommend "microdosing" initially, 2.5 to 5 milligrams, to see how it affects you, then waiting half a day. Since, legally, doctors have to give a recommendation and not a prescription, it's as close as we can get to providing a prescription.

Do you need to get a medical marijuana card in the seven states where cannabis is now fully legal?
Yes. There are a couple reasons you'd want to get a card. The best one: If you spend more than $100 a month, you'll save money with a tax break of at least 7.5 percent—even higher in some counties in California.

Can you buy medical marijuana at recreational dispensaries in states where pot is legal?
It varies. In Colorado, there are dispensaries just for medical and just for recreational, but in California and Nevada, most of the dispensaries are one-stop shops.

Many states allow you to grow your own if you have a card—which is how much marijuana, generally?
It differs by state and even by county. In California, some counties allow growing; some don't. Some states allow patients to grow plants—the number is typically anywhere from six to 12—but only some of those can be mature plants.

And how much can you possess?
It's all over the map, so to speak. Most states limit you to around 2.5 ounces of dried marijuana, California and Washington allow 8 ounces, while Oregon's limit is 24 ounces. Check your state's laws.

> 66
> **IN SOME STATES, YOU MUST HAVE A TERMINAL ILLNESS [TO GET A MEDICAL CARD]; BUT IN MANY STATES, CHRONIC PAIN OR PTSD WILL QUALIFY YOU."**
> **ROB TANKSON, CEO OF PRESTODOCTOR.COM**

What does a dried ounce typically cost in a dispensary?
It's a lot like wine: The higher the quality, the higher the cost. But you expect to pay about $30 to $35 for average quality. For higher-quality buds, the price can go up to $400 an ounce.

Concentrates like waxes and oils for vaping are $20 to $60 a gram. Edibles come in all kinds of foods now—pizza, burritos, ice cream, you name it—and cost about $3 to $5 per dose, but you don't need as much and they last longer. Liquid concentrates or tinctures, which you can put in foods or beverages, cost between $20 and $40 for a 1-ounce bottle.

Last question, are there any other pitfalls to consider with medical cannabis?
Your permit to carry a concealed firearm might be in jeopardy, but that varies from state to state. In Nevada, your concealed-carry permit will be revoked if you're listed on the state medical-marijuana registry, but that's not the case in New York, California or Oregon.

Typically, state law trumps federal law, but until the federal government reclassifies cannabis, there will always be some conflict. Also, many nationwide or global companies, like airlines, may have policies that prohibit marijuana use and will test for it.

Acupuncture, like cannabis, was once outside of the medical mainstream.

A WAKE-UP CALL FOR THE MEDICAL COMMUNITY

Patients are moving beyond the conventional model of pharmaceuticals.

An integrative cannabis physician with practices in California and New York, Junella Chin, DO, is an advocate for a better understanding of the science and medicine of marijuana. Medical cannabis and the science behind the endocannabinoid system are her specialities—and with the educational advantage of being schooled and based in California, a state that legalized medical cannabis in 1996, she was able to engineer her circumstances.

In her practice, she helps patients accept responsibility for maintaining their health through education and empowerment, and then, together, they decide how best to proceed in the context of their particular economic, environmental and lifestyle circumstances. "I encourage patients to really understand themselves," explains Dr. Chin, whose background includes conventional medicine but also nutritional training, osteopathy and acupuncture (another practice that was taboo not long ago).

"Patients should not be afraid to advocate for themselves in a way that is collaborative with their

Junella Chin, integrative cannabis physician

physician," Dr. Chin adds. Her belief is that the medical-cannabis movement should be a wake-up call to the health-care system. Dr. Chin is all about learning to unlearn and let go of outdated things: "In medical school, there is a 'this is how we've always done it' syndrome. That is the conventional, allopathic medicine model. How did we come to believe that prescription medication is the most effective way to treat disease?"

Her patients are looking for reliable information, but there are few trusted resources. This leaves them looking for advice from unconventional sources—which has a significant impact on doctors, who receive little or no education regarding medical cannabis.

When Dr. Chin first started, doctors were quiet about cannabis because of the stigma and regulation. Now, it's a mainstream topic, and she remains cautiously optimistic: "Cannabis is not a silver bullet. However, I believe CBD is a potent anti-inflammatory, and there is potential to springboard this into a preventive medical arena." Her idea of cannabis happiness? Legalization and FDA approval.

Tinctures

Vaping

Edibles

Candies

DO-IT-YOURSELF DOSING

What to know about finding the proper marijuana dosage for you.

For too many new medical marijuana users, home dosing can feel as daunting as being asked to chart their way through the Alaskan wilderness without a guide. It feels like you and you alone are responsible for gauging your symptoms, measuring effective doses and assessing any withdrawal. However, by keeping just a few simple tips in mind, experts say newcomers can demystify the process and ensure a positive experience.

First, take a look at all the different ways to consume cannabinoids (CBD), those mysterious and possibly pain-relieving chemicals that have made medical marijuana so popular. They come in lotions you can rub on your aching joints. They come in all kinds of foods, like gummy bears, cookies and sodas. They come in oils you can drop under your tongue. And, of course, they come from inhaling what's in the traditional bongs and joints. Once you've looked at all these options, it's important to decide which you're most comfortable taking into your body.

From there, make sure you're giving yourself a correct amount of cannabis. This has never been an exact science, going all the way back to that pot brownie you may have had in college. There was virtually no way to know how much THC (the chemical responsible for the "high" you get from marijuana) was infused in the butter it was made with, let alone where within the batch the THC was concentrated. Older users who grew up in an era of pot prohibition, long before medical use was in vogue, may still pass along urban legends about the strength of doses that flattened them as though they'd been hit by a truck.

STARTING OUT SMALL

Luckily, we live in an age now where precision is more possible. When you buy a product from a local dispensary, the dosage should be marked clearly on packages of oils and edibles. This allows users to start small. From there, it's important to pay attention to how your body reacts. As with any drug, everyone's body will respond differently, and one patient's ideal dose of 10 milligrams of THC could be double what might work for another.

If you're going to use medicinal marijuana at home, though, remember that this is not a quick fix. It could take time to figure out what will and won't work for you, explains Emma Chasen, director of education for the Sativa Science Club, a website designed to monitor the cannabis industry.

"The thing I really advocate for when you're learning what works for you is microdosing," says Chasen, referring to a process in which patients take a dose as low as 2 milligrams to start, especially if THC is involved. Since that is what creates the feeling of intoxication, starting very slow with it should provide the therapeutic benefits without any perceived high. This is especially important for patients who are prone to having feelings of anxiety.

Another thing that's critical if you're trying to treat yourself? Keeping a journal of how much you're using, as well as the conditions you use it under, the time of day you use it and the severity of symptoms you have before and after partaking in your pot. Doing this creates reliable documentation of your medical-marijuana sweet spot, that tipping point where your pain goes away but you don't feel like running out to a Grateful Dead concert.

Patience is most definitely a virtue when it comes to using

> **" DOSING IS DIFFERENT FOR EVERYONE. IT'S GOING TO DEPEND ON YOUR PHYSIOLOGY. I DEFINITELY ADVISE REACHING OUT TO A DOCTOR OR A HEALTH-AND-WELLNESS COACH."**
>
> **EMMA CHASEN, SATIVA SCIENCE CLUB**

marijuana. Maureen Dowd, a columnist at *The New York Times*, is a perfect example. She once wrote a story recounting an infamous, and highly avoidable, freak-out she had when she traveled to Colorado in 2014 to sample the state's newly legal edibles. Dowd ate an entire marijuana-infused chocolate bar, then spent the rest of the day melting down in her hotel room.

"As my paranoia deepened, I became convinced that I had died and no one was telling me," she wrote.

Experts will tell you that if Dowd had simply started with a small-dose edible—perhaps a 10 milligram gummy bear—and then consumed more if necessary, her experience would have been a much happier one. The key thing to remember from this example: Just because you don't feel the way you want to right away doesn't mean that you need to immediately add another dose. Give the compounds plenty of time to work.

KNOW WHAT YOU DON'T KNOW

Finally, advises Chasen, make sure to plan ahead if you're going to try medical marijuana. In particular, if it's your first home-dosing session, remember that you're still finding your level and anything is possible. This means

HOW TO AVOID ONLINE SCAMMERS

In a way, medical marijuana is the new Viagra. And no, not because it offers any particular help in that department. Rather, just as messages offering miracle erectile-dysfunction cures cluttered your email inbox after Viagra hit the market, messages promoting miracle cannabinoid cures are now coming in.

The subject lines have phrases like "Cannabidiol Oil Relieves Anxiety, Lowers Blood Sugar Levels." And since hemp is legal in the U.S., purchasers of CBD derived from hemp don't need to have a medical card. Thus, it's easier for questionable companies to peddle their wares. Not surprisingly, the flood of online cannabis offers has industry experts concerned.

"It's definitely becoming an issue," explains Debra Borchardt, CEO and editor-in-chief of the Green Market Report, an online newsletter focusing on cannabis financial news. "From what I've heard, many of the products making these claims actually have no CBD in them. It's a scam people should be aware of. If you're buying a product like this, you need to know the company and where it gets its cannabis."

Whom can you trust?
It might seem obvious to most consumers that a product seeming too good to be true most likely is. However, there's no need to assume that there's no medicinal value to any product being offered over the internet. You just need to understand what questions to ask before purchasing. It might seem natural to go to your physician for help, but that's not necessarily the most reliable approach.

"If you go to your doctor, that's awesome, but most of them don't know much about this world of medical marijuana and are reluctant to talk about it," explains Emma Chasen, director of education for the Sativa Science Club, a website designed to monitor the cannabis industry by providing instruction and networking opportunities. "You would probably be better off going to a naturopath or a nurse, either of whom might have more experience."

You could also seek firsthand accounts from friends or relatives, but their experiences will be anecdotal. That's why Chasen has this advice for anyone wanting to check on an online offer— or any cannabis provider, for that matter. "Get in touch with me. I'm happy to field questions. All this can be really intimidating, but the healing potential of cannabis is incredible. You just need someone to help navigate the muddy waters and show you what will be reliable and what won't."

that it's critical to schedule the experience for a window in your day when you can allow the marijuana to take effect without concern for having to travel or work. If you are an older patient who relies on any form of home care, it's also important that your caregiver understands your needs and dosage history (once you've established one).

And one more thing. While it should go without saying, Chasen cautions cannabis patients to avoid mixing their new meds with any other intoxicants, like alcohol. There's no telling how it will interact with the marijuana, and it's not worth taking a chance.

Ultimately, it all comes down to this for newcomers to home dosing: If they can just know it's OK to not know everything when they get started, they will ultimately be fine.

"As we move from prohibition to normalization, there's still a lot of misinformation out there—and, especially with older patients, there can be misunderstandings about how this works," Chasen says. "We're getting better, but I get a lot of questions about how dosing might interact with other medications. The truth is that for some drugs, we aren't sure of the interactions yet, because we don't have the research. So check in on yourself—keep a close watch on how your system feels and how you're responding."

> "AS WE MOVE FROM PROHIBITION TO NORMALIZATION, THERE'S STILL A LOT OF MISINFORMATION OUT THERE."
>
> **EMMA CHASEN**

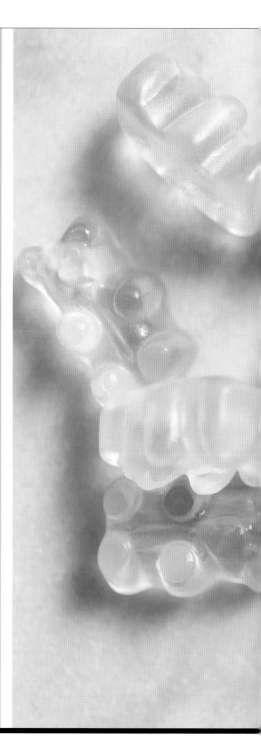

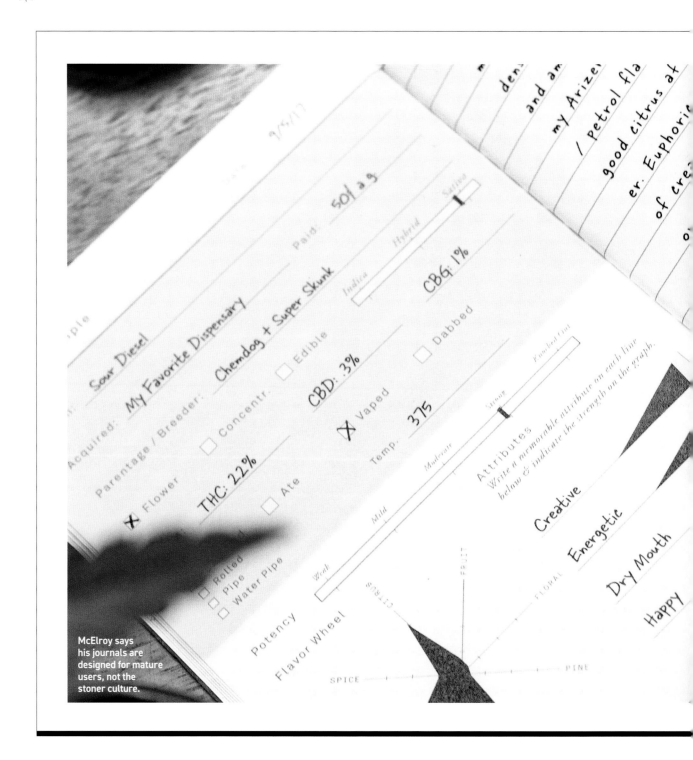

McElroy says his journals are designed for mature users, not the stoner culture.

THE WRITE STUFF

Journaling is a key ingredient in medical cannabis use.

There are plenty of things patients figure they'll no longer have to worry about when trying medical cannabis instead of prescription drugs—for instance, pain, addiction and over-the-top medication costs. However, there is one thing that they will have to contend with that traditional drug users don't: They have to be willing to write.

Medical-marijuana providers often insist patients keep a journal of their marijuana use because, at this point, dosing is an inexact science. Users need to keep track of what they take, how much they take and what effects they feel in order to get to the right place.

"This is useful for your caregiver or doctor because it can build a bridge between your own self-medication and their expert advice," says Charles McElroy, founder of Gold Leaf, a printing company that specializes in "science-forward" cannabis-related products, such as journals.

"This is incredibly important in today's cannabis industry, because there is no overarching system of reference or regulation. Patients are largely left to their own trials to determine what works best for them, and it is a challenge to always know exactly what you're getting."

That's why he created what he calls "the first patient-focused cannabis journal." McElroy's unique approach was to come up with a book that seemed simpler, more elegant and extremely user-friendly for beginners who feel intimidated by this new world and don't want something heavy with clinical or stoner-culture language.

"I'm hopeful that our journals will continue to be an accessible way for people to have good first experiences with cannabis," he explains. "I see a need in the industry for education and reference materials to help new users] better understand cannabis and their relationship with it.

Charles McElroy

Our journals, with their elegant and mature aesthetic, are something that many people who are new to cannabis find disarming—and people who are avid users find refreshing."

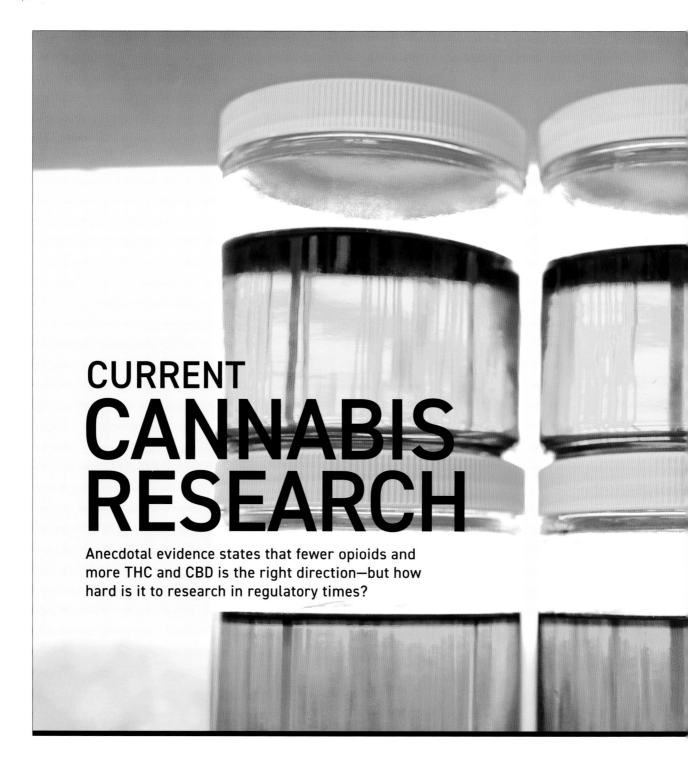

CURRENT
CANNABIS
RESEARCH

Anecdotal evidence states that fewer opioids and more THC and CBD is the right direction—but how hard is it to research in regulatory times?

The evidence is in: Cannabis has a role in preventing opioid use.

Conducting cannabis research involves interactions with several federal agencies: the National Institute on Drug Abuse (NIDA), to obtain the cannabis; the Food and Drug Administration (FDA), to receive an investigational new drug (IND) application; and the Drug Enforcement Administration (DEA), for an investigator registration and site licensure. While it's challenging to conduct research within this regulatory framework, there are processes in place—and conducting cannabinoid research may get easier with broader legislation to remove cannabis from the Controlled Substance Act (CSA) and bills like the Medical Marijuana Research Act.

In the meantime, for those who've found success, cannabis researchers talk about the plant's therapeutic promise but also emphasize how little we

Research on the use of marijuana to lower opioid use remains difficult due to marijuana's Schedule 1 classification.

know about its complexity. And while the FDA is aware that cannabis is being used for medical conditions (AIDS wasting, epilepsy, neuropathic pain, multiple sclerosis, cancer and chemotherapy-induced nausea, for example), it has not approved a marketing application for any indication. It has approved the cannabis-derived product Epidiolex, which contains purified cannabidiol (CBD) for the treatment of seizures associated with Lennox-Gastaut syndrome or Dravet syndrome in patients 2 years of age and older. The agency also has approved Marinol and Syndros for therapeutic uses, including for the treatment of the anorexia associated with weight loss in AIDS patients.

WHAT'S AHEAD

Scientists like Adie Wilson-Poe, PhD, an NIH-funded neuroscientist who studies cannabis, opioids and their interaction, are dedicated to ensuring that cannabis research goes mainstream so that the future of medical cannabis is for all, and widely applied.

Her hypothesis: If we use cannabinoids, we can reduce reliance on opioids and lessen their dangerous side effects. In other words: Relieve pain with cannabis while lowering reliance on dangerous drugs. Wilson-Poe's work has shown that cannabinoids enhance the pain-relieving effects of opioids and that they may also prevent the development of opioid tolerance. These results, and those of her colleagues in a rapidly growing scientific field, suggest that cannabis can keep people from increasing their opioid use over time, thus preventing opioid dependence and misuse. She believes that the compelling nature of the existing data and the relative safety profile of cannabis warrants further exploration of cannabis treatment. However, without a fundamental characterization of pain neurobiology and the interaction between chronic pain and the brain's reward system, alleviating the opioid epidemic is challenging. So her research begins there.

CHRONIC PAIN

To start, what is chronic pain? "While the world's leading experts argue about the nuances of the definition," says Wilson-Poe, "most can agree that chronic pain is when acute pain [a broken wrist, a surgery or a car accident, for example] resolves itself but there is still a lingering effect for six months or longer."

Wilson-Poe goes on to explain that the coadministration of opioids and cannabinoids could provide better pain relief than the consumption of either drug alone. Findings indicate that alternating opioid and cannabinoid treatment could be a safer and more

Adie Wilson-Poe, PhD

"

MY LONG-TERM GOAL: TO CHARACTERIZE THE HARM-REDUCING ROLE OF CANNABIS IN THE OPIOID CRISIS."

ADIE WILSON-POE, PHD

sustainable pain-relief option than the long-term administration of opioids on their own.

Wilson-Poe finds it most relevant to women, as they experience more chronic pain. She mentions neuropathy—the malfunction of peripheral nerves from diabetes or chemotherapy, for example—and fibromyalgia, characterized by musculoskeletal pain, fatigue, sleep, memory and mood issues, which amplifies pain by affecting the way the brain processes pain signals.

"Thanks to research by my colleagues," says Wilson-Poe, "we know that the cannabis experience is profoundly impacted by the biological sex of the organism. It's important to fully characterize these sex differences so that we don't jump to the wrong conclusions when it comes to cannabis therapy." Her latest NIH grant, funded by the National Institute on Drug Abuse, is assessing these sex differences in the context of opioid tolerance and chronic pain.

Reports on cannabis benefits for pain have been anecdotal (for more than 5,000 years), community defined (where a group of people report) and backed by peer-reviewed evidence. Now Wilson-Poe can research, document and move medicine toward scientifically based cannabis treatments.

Per the CDC, about 130 Americans die every day from opioid overdoses.

OPTING OUT OF OPIOIDS

Overwhelmed by painkillers, a nurse finds hope in cannabis.

I t was pain that drove Debbie Mayberry to become a nurse. She decided to take up her medical career after losing her newborn son to a congenital heart defect and caring for her grandmother through several health crises. Then, just when she'd achieved her dream of helping her patients get through their agony, she had even more pain to deal with.

In 2011, she slipped and injured her back during a hospital work shift. Suddenly, despite her many years of clinical experience, she wasn't able to nurse herself back to health and a pain-free life. She couldn't work and ended up bedridden, thanks to debilitating pain and depression. Her only source of comfort was a growing array of opioids prescribed for relief.

OVERWHELMED BY "HORRIBLE" DRUGS

For someone with so much experience dispensing pain meds, Mayberry never saw her own dependency coming. The OxyContin that her workers' compensation doctor originally prescribed left her unable to function, prompting her to write a scathing letter to him, complaining that "such a horrible drug" left her unable to drive, let alone return to her job.

"He 'fired' me as a patient. He said I was noncompliant: 'If you're not going to take the medication I'm going to prescribe, I can't help you,'" recalls Mayberry.

She then went to her own doctor, who wasn't any more helpful. The physician prescribed Percocet for daily use and advised Mayberry that her nursing career was over. Feeling like she had no other choice, she filed for short- and long-term disability. Things got even worse when she lost her workers' compensation claim because her preexisting fibromyalgia, not her fall, was seen as the cause of her persistent pain.

Mayberry reapplied for short- and long-term disability, and her doctor started prescribing a medicine cabinet's worth of pharmaceuticals: Ativan for sleep; Savella for fibromyalgia; Neurontin for neuropathy; oxycodone for pain from bulging

> ## 66
> ## I WASN'T TRYING TO CHECK OUT. I WAS TRYING TO PARTICIPATE IN LIFE."
> **DEBBIE MAYBERRY**

discs and spinal-nerve-root compression; Efflexor for depression. Mayberry began to realize she'd become the sort of painkiller user she would never have let her own patients become. If she missed taking her antidepressants, she flew into uncontrollable rages. After going 36 hours without Ativan because she'd forgotten to get her prescription filled, she recalls being 'in tears, nonfunctional. I told my doctor, 'This is seriously not OK. You've got me on all these medications. I'm dependent.'"

Frustrated by her doctor's reluctance to help her ease out of opioid use and uncertain what else was available to treat her condition, Mayberry was desperate. So, when a friend who was using FECO (full extract cannabis oil) to treat interstitial lung disease suggested in 2014 that Mayberry "stop all that s--t and use cannabis," she decided to give it a try. Over the next two years, she slowly but surely began to wean herself from opioid dependency, reclaiming her sanity, health and recovery.

Mayberry began using cannabis oil, putting it in food or taking it in capsule form. "I used all components of the plant, getting a full host of endocannabinoids. It was helping my pain, and it was legal. I was getting my cannabis by doing marijuana-trimming work

For many, CBD works as well as opioids to lessen pain.

[for growers]; in exchange, they would give me cannabis oil or the cannabis flower—and I could make my own."

SLOW-BUT-STEADY SUCCESS

She soon learned which strains worked for her situation, based on what her growers had available. Some, Mayberry recalls, "were better for getting up and working and having energy and feeling motivated. Others helped me relax at night. They all helped with pain."

But she has discovered that CBD alone isn't enough to ease all that ails her.

"I need the THC because it helps with my mood and helps with my pain," Mayberry explains. "I cook with it. I make infused butter. I smoke as well, when I'm in a place that's appropriate to do that. Even with pharmaceuticals, I always tried to take the least possible so I could participate in life. I wasn't trying to check out. I wanted to participate."

The plan worked. She carefully kept weaning herself off most of the drugs she'd been taking. "I had tapered down to 10mg [of oxycodone] or less daily, so I just stopped. My prescription ran out,

and I said, 'I'm done.' I was doing really well with pain. I was up and around, able to do things. I still had pain, but I just felt better."

These days, since retiring from nursing, she hopes to become an activist and educator in order to change the public's perception of those in the treatment community, and work to convince them that cannabis is a healthy, viable alternative to opioids. Says Mayberry, "Change is so slow. I happen to be able to speak up now [about medical marijuana] because I come from a nursing background and can talk with conviction."

Family
Values

Although it can
be uncomfortable,
the weed talk is
a must. Kids need
to know the facts.

THE TALK

How to speak with your kids about cannabis
before they hear the wrong information.
(Hint: Be a good listener; make good choices.)

Do you remember the first time your mom sat you down for The Talk? From her serious face and tone, you could tell it was going to be a doozy. Possible topics? Sex, drugs or alcohol. Pot, usually lumped into the taboo drug group, was perceived as a societal danger and challenged belief systems. And, at the end of the day, it was illegal.

While no one is suggesting that parents condone recreational cannabis use with their children, the world is changing—and maybe The Talk needs to as well. Here are a few ideas for how to discuss marijuana with your kids.

KEEP IT SIMPLE

If you have young children between the ages of 6 and 9, the conversation should start with the basics and how nature supports human life: fresh water, air, sunshine, fruits and vegetables, all kinds of plants that can be used for medicine, clothing, building, etc. This includes cannabis and hemp.

KEEP IT REAL

If you have middle or high schoolers, myth-bust first. There's a lot of misinformation coming from old-paradigm-thinking educators and this could lead down a dangerous path.

MYTH Marijuana is a gateway drug.

TRUTH Marijuana is the most popular and easily accessible illegal drug in the U.S. today. So people who have used less-accessible drugs (heroin, cocaine, LSD) are likely to have first accessed marijuana and other more accessible drugs, including alcohol. But many experts say the use of one does not cause the use of another.

MYTH Today's marijuana is the same as when I was a kid.

TRUTH The marijuana available today is the same plant that has been used for thousands of years. Due to the large number of marijuana varieties, however, the level of THC—the main psychoactive ingredient—varies. Interestingly, marijuana tested in areas where it is illegal tends to be stronger. Why? Because when access to a particular substance is sporadic, risky and limited, both consumers and producers are incentivized to use or sell higher-potency material. There was a similar trend during Prohibition. Beer and cider were largely replaced by spirits and hard liquor, which were easier and more profitable to transport. When access is regulated and controlled, as in states where medical marijuana is legal, we see a wider variety of potencies, including marijuana with virtually no traces of THC but high in cannabidiol (CBD), which is therapeutic but not psychoactive. Different methods of ingestion can also affect the strength of marijuana. Marijuana-infused edibles, for example, can have a stronger intoxicating effect and last longer than smoking. It's important to regulate dosage and remember that it can take up to one hour before a marijuana edible takes effect.

MYTH Using marijuana has long-term effects on the brain.

TRUTH Whether you've tried it yourself or been with someone under the influence, you know that "getting high" can change how a person thinks and behaves. Some short-term effects may include immediate changes in thoughts, perceptions and information processing. The cognitive process most clearly affected by marijuana is short-term memory, but this usually disappears as soon as the person is no longer intoxicated. So what about the long term? There's no convincing evidence that even heavy, long-term marijuana use by adults permanently impairs memory or other cognitive functions. Some studies have shown that heavy marijuana use starting in the early teens has an impact on the area of the brain responsible for memory, while other studies have shown no impact. What is clear is that much more research is needed. It is strongly recommended that teens not use marijuana, since their brains are still developing—and, in particular, the part of the brain that controls emotional development can be sensitive.

MYTH Cannabis kills.

TRUTH Cannabis doesn't kill. According to the Drug Enforcement Administration (DEA) drug data sheet on marijuana: "No death from overdose of marijuana has been reported." When abused, alcohol, opiates and traditional prescriptions do kill. According to the Centers for Disease Control, 130 Americans, on average, die daily from an opioid overdose.

MYTH All marijuana is equally bad.

TRUTH Recreational use of high-THC strains, synthetic weed/fweed (fake weed), street pot, K2, kratom (a plant with withdrawal symptoms that can be as painful as those of opiates), etc. is dangerous. They are designed for maximum addiction, to keep

Find a quiet time
to have a weed talk
with your kids.

121

Teach your children to make informed choices.

THE DO'S AND DON'TS
OF CANNABIS AND PARENTING

DO

→ Educate yourself
→ Be honest and open
→ Communicate constantly
→ Emphasize the difference
  between recreational and
  medical use
→ Watch your kids for signs
  of misuse

DON'T

→ Believe what you see, read
  or hear. Authenticate, verify
  and validate all information;
  your kid will go online
→ Lie
→ Pretend to be a friend;
  you should be the trusted
  adult/role model

consumers brand-loyal, and include a host of toxic chemicals, volatile compounds and even traces of mold.

TO USE PLANTS WELL, WE MUST USE THEM WISELY.

Teens are going to experiment with marijuana (one in five is the national average) and from that, many recognize that it can help with sleep, anxiety and depression as well as aid in focus. Compared with the side effects of prescription drugs, new studies have suggested that cannabis can safely support teens, but any medicinal use should be under the care of a licensed doctor in a legal state. It is not advisable for teens to self-medicate or use marijuana

inappropriately, especially while their brains are still developing.

SO...WHAT IF YOU PARTAKE?

As a parent and an adult, what you choose to use for recreation or as medicine does not entitle your child to do the same. And, whether you yourself use is irrelevant. What *is* relevant is that your teen learns to make decisions based on fact, health, wellness and lifestyle—not from TV or friends. Talk about the distinction, and set appropriate boundaries.

Be honest and educate. Then, when your child asks, you will have the keys to successfully manage the conversation—no matter how uncomfortable it may be.

Weed and the American Family

The headline stats of a Yahoo! News-Marist Poll (released in April 2017) speak to how many parents have tried marijuana and use it regularly.

52%
of Americans (18+) have tried marijuana at some point in their lives

65%
are parents—that's about 83,747,495 parents

22%
of American adults use marijuana, and 63 percent of this group say they use it regularly

44%
of those individuals who have tried it currently use it

Among Americans who use marijuana:

30% are parents with children younger than 18 (about 16,353,060 parents with underage children)

54% are parents (about 29,435,508 parents)

Among Americans who regularly use marijuana:

51% are parents—about 17,691,033 people

27% are parents with children younger than 18 years of age (or about 9,365,841 parents with underage children)

25% of women who use marijuana say they use it while pregnant, according to the American College of Obstetrics and Gynecology

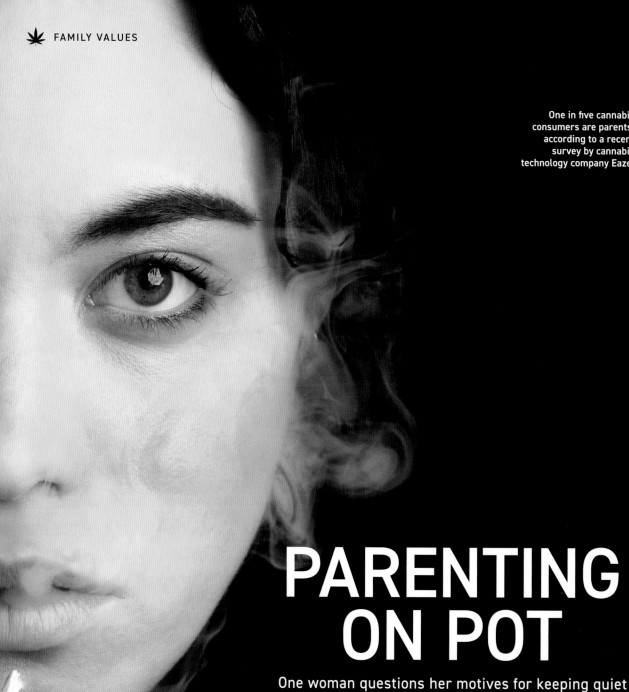

One in five cannabis consumers are parents, according to a recent survey by cannabis technology company Eaze.

PARENTING ON POT

One woman questions her motives for keeping quiet about cannabis use but soon finds that she is not alone.

There's no telling what I might have accomplished this week had I been stoned, but I know what I didn't. I didn't shower for two days, because I didn't feel like clearing the tub of my children's bath toys to make way for my feet. I didn't ask them to pick up the toys, because they'd never squeeze the water out properly. I didn't get it on with my husband, mostly because I couldn't stop thinking about the overdue bills that were piled on the desk—but he'll tell you it's because I hadn't showered. I also didn't grocery-shop, because I forgot my reusable tote and marine life is dying from plastic in the ocean.

What, you might ask, does this hamster wheel of errands have to do with me getting high? Marijuana for me is not a means to escape. It's a way to relax and be grounded, to exist within myself and quiet some of the noise that makes me less present for everyone else. When I'm not showering, it's not only toys to blame. It's the pile on the desk I have to pass on my way to the bathtub taking my focus. It's the food I keep thinking about, that I didn't buy, that I'm making a mental list to grab tomorrow. It's the reusable tote I jumped up from the homework table to shove into my purse so history won't repeat itself.

"I absolutely have to be high if I want to play with my kids," a dear friend and mother of two boys told me. "The only way for me to engage and block out all my responsibilities and distractions is to smoke. Plus pushing trains on a track is really boring."

So it is true for most of the demands of motherhood. Unlike full-time working parents, at-home moms never escape the minutiae of parenthood. Housework is squeezed in a hectic vice of getting kids to school and then retrieving them.

It's a race for breakfast (which will be cleaned later) then snacks (no nuts, no seeds), then homework, playdates, dinner on the table by 6 o'clock, baths, books...it's patience, empathy, authoritarian, caregiving...and then we drop everything to be adults.

In our parents' less cyberspeed day, they unwound with a cocktail. Today, it's a puff. And unlike the inebriation that comes with drunkenness, getting high makes me more present.

Almost every mom I spoke to referred to pot in parenting as something of a salve. "It's not that I'm high," said the mom of a first-grade girl on New York City's Upper East Side. "It's more like I'm breathing deeply."

Why, then, is there such stigma for a mom who gets stoned? Why is there no #marijuanamonday popping up like #winewednesday? Why is it not an option on the school potluck sign-up sheet, listed between beer and wine and (nut-free) brownies?

"You can get arrested for smoking pot!" said a rural mom of three to me recently. "People around here will chat about the best routes if you drive after drinking—but you pull out a vape pen, and the room goes silent." And that's actually the reason. Unlike alcohol, which is legal to buy and sell and ingest, pot simply isn't.

Every parent I know who indulges in marijuana use seems to have a restriction on when and how they use it. "In my home, one parent is stoned at a time," one dad told me. "This way, if the kids wake up or there is an emergency, one of us is can address it sober and safely."

"In our house, it's just a question of making sure the kids are asleep," said the Upper East Side mom. "We live in New York City. We can hail a cab if there's an emergency. And if our daughter wakes up, she's in the adjacent room of the apartment."

Which makes me wonder if my puff isn't as radical as it seems. In fact, maybe my puff will get the bathroom cleaned, the kids to school and my marriage back on track.

—Kate Botta

Roughly 10,000 people turn 65 each day in the U.S., with many seeking safer, cheaper ways to relieve pain.

THE FAMILY PLAN

As more older Americans turn to cannabis,
they are searching for a way to explain the choice to their kids.

With recreational use of cannabis legal in 10 states now, and fully functioning medical cannabis programs in 23 more, there's no doubt that people are talking about cannabis. Still, there's at least one group that has remained silent on the issue: families. The long-standing stigma associated with marijuana continues to make it hard for older parents to tell their adult children that they want (or need) to use weed.

To learn how to kick-start those difficult conversations, we spoke with etiquette expert Lizzie Post, the great-great-granddaughter of Emily Post, the original arbiter of proper manners. Based in Vermont, where she works as co-president of the Emily Post Institute, Lizzie is a proud cannabis consumer who's written seven books on etiquette, including her latest, *Higher Etiquette: A Guide to the World of Cannabis, From Dispensaries to Dinner Parties.* Here is her advice on how families can come together when it comes to cannabis.

Q How do older people who've told their kids to "just say no" their whole lives now admit to them they want to smoke cannabis?
Take a minute to think why you want to add it to your lifestyle, then you'll be able to have that conversation with your kids from a perspective of, this is a thoughtful choice I'm making, not just something I'm randomly doing. Be intentional about it.

Q Do you believe that you even have to tell them?
No, you don't. If your kids are out of the house, it's your own business, so first I would decide whether you need to or want to share that information. Now, if they're

coming for a visit with the grandkids and you think you'll want to consume in a way that will be noticeable, like smoking a joint, then you might say, "Hey, listen. There is something different about my lifestyle now. I've started smoking pot, so we should probably talk about what's going to be comfortable and what isn't." Basically, it really just depends on whether the consumption of cannabis will happen with others around, particularly children.

Every family is entitled to feel comfortable in their own home, but so are your guests. The gamut of solutions could run from having your children and grandchildren stay in a hotel or Airbnb if your use in front of them makes them uncomfortable, to you abstaining and locking everything away. It really just depends on the viewpoints that your children hold and how much you want to accommodate them. Etiquette isn't going to tell you which one is right, but etiquette does say you should feel comfortable in your own home and your guests should be comfortable when they come to visit.

Lizzie Post spent four months on the road researching her new book about weed etiquette.

Q Is it easier to tell them a little white lie by saying it's for medicinal use?

I really try to encourage people not to feel the judgment from others. I know for me, when I present it to someone as a very positive aspect of my life, I don't feel judged as much as I have when I've sheepishly apologized for it and say, "Oh, yeah, I still smoke pot." What's wrong with still smoking pot? Why does it have to be something I only did in college? I found people will view it in a negative light, as well. But when I say, "My experience with cannabis has been really positive. It's something that I noticed allows me to focus more, or turns the volume down on my reactions a little bit." When I start in that kind of way, the questions become, "OK, so who do you do it with? What do you like to do when you get high? Is it all day, every day?" I find they get curious rather than judgmental.

Q How do adults tell their younger children they consume cannabis?

In states where it's legal, it's a discussion you have just like you do with alcohol, cigarettes, sex or firearms. There are adult things that are really good to talk to kids about, and when they're an adult, they can make those decisions, too. Use it as a teaching moment to educate them about the pros and cons of it.

> 66
> **TAKE A MINUTE TO THINK WHY YOU WANT TO ADD (CANNABIS) TO YOUR LIFESTYLE. THEN YOU'LL BE ABLE TO HAVE THAT CONVERSATION WITH YOUR KIDS."**
> **LIZZIE POST**

Q How would your great-great-grandmother feel about the book?

She'd be all for it. One of the more surprising things about Emily's personality was that she really fought hard against Prohibition. She campaigned against it. She did not believe it was OK for the government to infringe upon citizens' rights and their choice to drink alcohol even though she herself didn't drink. We feel that this book falls right in line with her thinking on that—although she didn't approve of smoking, so I don't think she would approve of her great-great-granddaughter's love of joints. But she would defend my right to engage with it legally while also taking other people's boundaries, perspectives and comfort levels into consideration.

In Colorado, 36 percent of those on the state's medical cannabis registry are 50 or older.

GETTING THE GREEN IN YOUR GOLDEN YEARS

Compared to their younger peers, fewer older people are currently trying marijuana. The best estimate of use by those 50 to 64 ranges from 5.6 percent to 9.1 percent, according to a 2018 study by the National Institutes of Health. Meanwhile, for those 65 and older, that figure drops to between 1.3 percent and 2 percent. However, the greatest increase in marijuana use has also been observed in older folks. From 2006 to 2013, marijuana use among those 50 or older jumped significantly, up 71.4 percent, with the largest percentage increase coming from those 65 or older. Most reported using cannabis to treat pain, anxiety, loss of appetite and/or weight loss, depression and insomnia rather than for recreational reasons. While men were more likely to use marijuana than women, marijuana use in females doubled from 2006 to 2013.

131

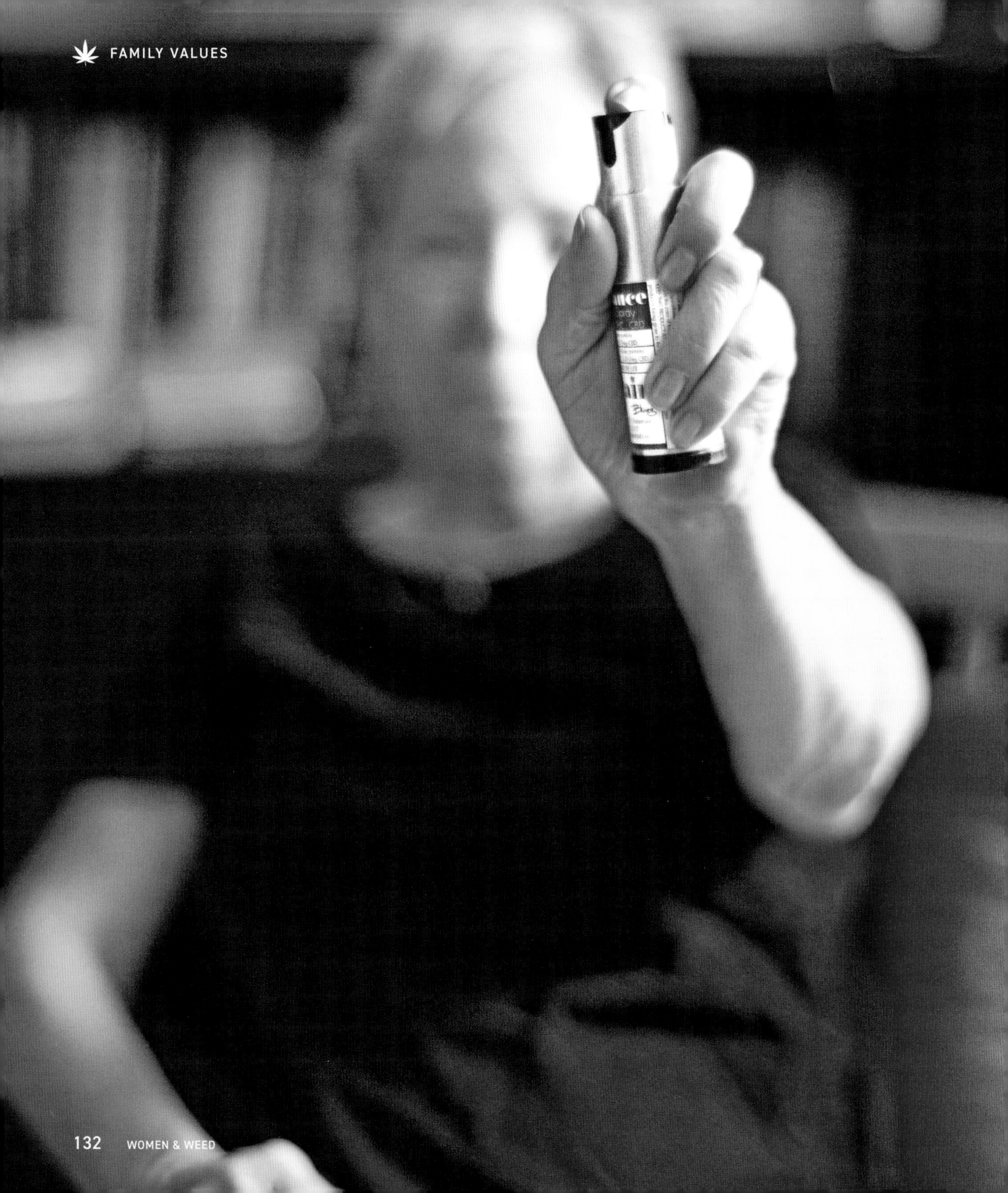

MY MEDICAL-MARIJUANA JOURNEY

At 72 years old, after some trepidation and fear, I found out that cannabis simply provided relief.

On Friday, I had a bout of ischemic colitis. Friday night, there was blood. Early Saturday morning, my husband and I went to the ER. After a long day of tests, the radiologist said: "There is something else. You have ovarian cancer." It didn't compute. My husband and I were silent on the way home.

As a psychologist, with years of postdoctoral training, I have learned that I can focus on only one aspect of a problem at a time and only in chronological order. With everything happening at once, I was overwhelmed but pledged to listen and learn...but I was scared. I noticed that I held my breath—a lot.

What followed was an enormous blur and an intense physical, mental and emotional strain: a full hysterectomy, removal of a small cancer adjacent to the lining of the liver and a quarter-size tumor on my diaphragm. And a long recovery.

When the physician assistant (PA) outlined the next stage, which included chemotherapy infusions for the next five months, I was exhausted, fearful and still held my breath. My daughter asked about medical marijuana. The PA said that many patients find it helpful for pain, nausea and anxiety. I timidly asked for a prescription, and off we went.

I'd had very little experience with marijuana as a kid in suburban New York in the '50s and '60s. There was no misunderstanding of it, there were no scary images—it just wasn't part of my world. (Well, there was that one time that the boys at a 10th grade dance were "on" something and happily boisterous in the corner of the dance floor.) However, when my daughter told me her story, I listened. Cannabis had helped her recover from a traumatic brain injury (TBI).

So I applied for and received a New York State

full spectrum

CBD oil

ORGANIC
NON-GMO

DIETARY SUPPLEMENT
1 fl. oz. / 30ml / 300mg

Medical Marijuana Registry Identification Card. Now what?

My daughter became my cannabis caregiver. She went with me to "a reliable medical-marijuana dispensary that offers the best-quality medical-marijuana products to the patients of New York State," as the website put it. It never occurred to me to ask friends for recommendations. I was too nervous to tell anyone what I was doing. I still held my breath.

The dispensary, owned and operated by women, was welcoming. The pharmacist explained that a balanced dosage of CBD and THC was prescribed and should help me get through treatment: the CBD for the nausea; the THC for the anxiety. Then I had to choose a form. Vape pen? Too complicated. Drops under the tongue? Terrible taste. Spray with peppermint? "Like Binaca?" I asked. Done.

The pharmacist encouraged me to try out the dosage before the next chemotherapy infusion. So, right there, in her office, I sprayed. What happened next has become family legend. My daughter and I went to lunch, and I ordered an avocado salad.
Me: "Mmmmm, this avocado tastes soooooooo good."
My daughter: "Do you think the spray is having an effect?"
Me: "No, it's just a good avocado."
My daughter: "Really..."
The use of medical marijuana was

helpful throughout the chemo process. Only once did I feel nauseated, and that was after a long night's sleep without any medication. Otherwise, I went through treatment and worked with a sense of calm and focus.

NOW I KNOW THE TRUTH

I know that I am lucky. I had family support, financial means and access to good insurance and legal cannabis. Today, if someone asks, I encourage cancer patients to make use of medical marijuana, if legal in their state. And as for my friends... when someone asks how I made it through chemo while working, I simply say, with a quiet smile: "My family, my friends, my wonderful doctors, a positive attitude and medical marijuana." Then I exhale.
—*Lynne Blum*

> **"**
> **MEDICAL-MARIJUANA USE AMONG SENIORS IS ON THE RISE, AND NOW I UNDERSTAND WHY."**
> **LYNNE BLUM**

CBD UNLEASHED

Pet owners are increasingly turning
to cannabis to treat their ailing animals.

Cannabis and hemp may provide relief for pet stress.

T he current health-care crisis isn't just affecting the human members of families across the country. It's also hitting the ones covered with fur pretty hard. According to the American Pet Products Association, people spent an estimated $70 billion on medical treatments for their four-legged friends in 2017. With pet health-care costs expected to continue climbing, it's likely that dog and cat owners will keep turning to preventive treatments to help their animals. And, given its current popularity with people, it also makes sense that those treatments will include CBD.

According to Dr. Tim Shu, founder of VETCBD, which sells a variety of CBD products specifically formulated for household critters, cannabidiol can be effective for pets in the same way it benefits their humans. That's because people and their vertebrate cousins are born with the same endogenous cannabinoid system, which is made of both cell-produced endocannabinoids and cannabinoid receptors. CBD targets these receptors—located in the brain, organs, central nervous system and immune cells—to stimulate each body function's natural job, which is to promote healing, well-being and overall health.

Given this similarity between humans and animals, it's not surprising there seems to be nearly as many CBD-infused items for pets these days as there are for people. From vet-tested tinctures and oils to doggy treats, vitamin supplements, topical rubs and shampoos, hemp-derived products for animals are so popular that sales are expected to reach more than $125 million by 2022.

Despite this trend, organizations like the American Society for the Prevention of Cruelty to Animals have not yet endorsed CBD for pets. On its website, the ASPCA notes that "there are very few scientific studies looking at the efficacy and safety of CBD use in companion animals." Still, says an enthusiastic Shu, "It's an exciting time. Remember, the endocannabinoid system was only

> ❝
> **THANKS TO CBD-OIL DOG TREATS, WE'VE GONE FROM HAVING OUR DOG BUTTERBEAN BEING ANXIOUS IN THE CAR TO US ASKING, 'HEY, DID YOU KNOW THERE'S A DOG IN THE CAR?'"**
>
> **PET OWNER JOHN DOHERTY**

discovered in the 1990s and we're learning more and more every day. We're making strides in supporting everything like mood, memory, sleep, appetite and reproduction. The more we learn, the more our patients benefit, whether they walk on two legs or four. We're really just scratching the surface."

Shu and many other animal experts are high on the use of CBD for several conditions, particularly these:

◼ SEIZURES AND EPILEPSY

Roughly 5 percent of dogs in the U.S. suffer from seizures of one sort or another. While there's nothing conclusive as of yet, researchers believe high levels of CBD have shown promise in the management of your furry friend's seizures. Long-term therapy has indicated there's a reduction in frequency, and, in some cases, a complete elimination of them.

◼ CANINE AND FELINE ARTHRITIS

As many pet owners have learned, larger cat and dog breeds are prone to arthritis. Fortunately, CBD has been showing the same effectiveness in treatment for pets as it has for humans, since its anti-inflammatory properties target the inflammation of joints that

Veterinarians aren't covered under laws allowing doctors to recommend cannabis.

causes the debilitating illness, as well as its accompanying pain. The good news for your pooch is that a landmark study conducted by a Cornell University-led team of researchers tested hemp-oil products on dogs and found that 80 percent of them saw significant decrease in pain and improved mobility.

SEPARATION ANXIETY

As is apparent in their faces when we say goodbye every morning, dogs are particularly prone to anxiety when their owners are away. Many pet owners use prescription medications to treat them, but according to two different independent reports, the two approved antidepressants for canine separation anxiety can produce vomiting and lethargy in between 45 and 85 percent of the animals that use it. CBD may be a safer option for this condition, as well as with the general anxiety that comes from traveling and hearing loud noises.

A MOTHER'S FIGHT

How four moms are saving their children with the help of cannabis.

Tracy Ryan says daughter Sophie's tumor began shrinking two months after starting with CBD.

"THERE IS FINALLY SUPPORT FOR PEDIATRIC CANNABIS USE."

Tracy Ryan's life changed in the blink of an eye. Literally.

In 2013, she'd noticed a shaking in 8-and-a-half-month-old daughter Sophie's left eyeball. A chain of doctors' appointments later, Tracy was informed that her baby girl had an optic pathway glioma, a slow-growing tumor that can cause cancer and, in some cases, death. Chemotherapy was the only option for treatment.

The type of tumor Sophie suffered from had a survival rate of 90 percent but also a recurrence rate of 85 percent. As the Ryans searched for any alternatives for Sophie, they connected with TV host Ricki Lake, who was making a documentary about the use of cannabis oil for pediatric diseases. That led to Sophie starting on cannabis oils as well as chemotherapy, which drastically improved her condition.

The experience not only saved the girl's life, it also inspired Tracy to start CannaKids, a California cooperative corporation that provides information as well as medicinal cannabis oils to ill children and adults. She spoke with us about her journey and how she's translated the trauma into a triumph.

"The wrenching desperation led me, my husband and Sophie on a roller-coaster ride of despair and discovery, of cancer and chemotherapy and, most surprising, of cannabis. At first, Sophie's neurosurgeon told us that we needed to prepare for full blindness. There was a 100 percent chance of her losing sight in her left eye, and, best-case scenario, she would have minimal vision in her right eye," Tracy says.

"IT NEEDS TO STOP NOW"

"When I first started this process, I was lucky enough to meet Ricki Lake and [her producing partner] Abby Epstein, who were making a documentary about using cannabis oil to treat pediatric illnesses. They were able to really guide me through and bring me oils. I think it was around $7,000 of free oils they had, originally, for another little girl, who'd left to go to a legal state. I was lucky enough to get those.

"There are children in this optic pathway glioma group that I'm a member of on Facebook, who have literally been in chemotherapy for 13 years. So, again, this is why I'm so passionate about working with universities and other very respected pediatric hospitals

> **"**
> **IT'S REALLY UNFORTUNATE THAT WE HAVE TO DEAL WITH MANY OF THE HURDLES WE ARE CURRENTLY FACING."**
>
> **TRACY RYAN, CANNAKIDS**

around the country. I can get answers for my child and I can get research going in Israel on her brain-tumor sample. I can get answers for my kid so that she doesn't have to be one of those kids who goes through 13 years of chemotherapy. That sort of thing needs to stop, and it needs to stop now.

"Honestly, other patients are dying. If a child gets cancer in Jamaica, that child is sent home with a morphine drip if the parents can't afford the out-of-pocket expense of chemotherapy. It's very, very sad to see some of these regions and what these patients are going through—but it's also enlightening to see that their governments are getting behind them...and getting behind cannabis.

"And it is really unfortunate that we have to deal with many of the hurdles we have to deal with currently and the federal regulations that are putting up roadblocks. Our government is going to have to get onboard. We are supposed to be the greatest country in the world, yet we are exponentially behind on this initiative.

"Recently, though, I have to say the conversation really is changing. There was an article published on forbes.com titled "Medical Marijuana for Children With Cancer Is Broadly Supported by Doctors." This just goes to show how far we've come in six years' time, since we started this with Sophie. Back then, cannabis was a medicine that doctors had never heard of for children. They had heard of it for glaucoma, for pain or as a drug to get high. But now the masses are really supporting cannabis for pediatric use—and especially for pediatric research.

"Recent results we're seeing for autism are absolutely incredible. I can safely say this is, hands-down, the area in which we've had the most success. It's a really wonderful, beautiful thing when you have a child who was very violent and self-injurious, and they're smiling, happy, giving hugs and letting people touch them, and they haven't had a violent rage— we saw a child that hadn't had a violent rage in two years, who before was not even able to go to school. You can help with a lot of the side effects of autism, which can really create havoc in a family, and everyday life as a whole.

CREATING CANNAKIDS
"That's why we're so excited about human trials starting now on autism with nonpsychoactive THCA—the 'a' stands for acid. It's like juicing the raw plant, essentially. The therapeutic value that we're seeing in THCA and CBDA, which has a lot of new reporting behind it, is amazing. We're really trying to get that message out there as well.

"When I started down this path, I had so many people say to me, 'Do not call your company CannaKids. Do not start screaming about pediatric cancer and giving kids pot. They're going to come and take your kid and throw you in jail.' But I just instinctively had this feeling: I can't sit by and keep what I've experienced a secret. I can't sit by and let families suffer. I cannot be afraid of what's going to happen to

RYAN'S DAUGHTER SOPHIE, NOW 7, WAS DIAGNOSED WITH A BRAIN TUMOR BEFORE HER FIRST BIRTHDAY.

Tracy (seen here with Sophie and husband Josh), can now take her daughter on her speaking tours.

me, because I believe I'm here for a purpose. My daughter is here for a purpose. And I'm not going to let fear stand in the way of trying to help others. And I'm so happy that I've been able to do this, because it's what initially led me to say yes to everything that we've done since Sophie got sick.

A STRONGER, SMILING SOPHIE
"As for her current health, Sophie has another MRI scheduled. She goes to chemo every two weeks, with no side effects from the chemotherapy. The cannabis is not affecting her blood count for the protocol that she's on. She's also in school now; we can't take her out, so she's not traveling as much.

"Whenever she can, though, Sophie comes with me when I travel to speak. She has her own suitcase with wheels that she pulls though the airport. She has her own business cards. When the plane takes off, she says that it tickles her belly. She loves the snacks. She loves watching the movies. She loves napping on the airplane. She's literally the best little travel companion you could ever imagine. Sophie goes all over with me. She and I were at the TMC Innovation Institute, at Texas Medical Center, in Houston. We were speaking at an event, and I brought her up onstage with me at the very end, as I do whenever she travels with me.

"Sophie stepped up to the stage and looked up at me with these big, blue eyes and said, 'Mommy, can I say something?' And I said, 'Of course, you can, honey.' So, she grabbed the microphone from my hand, unprompted, unrehearsed, and said, 'Hi, my name is Sophie, and I take cannabis...' She just brought down the house!

"Sophie was so healthy and vivacious, so energetic—running all around the TMC Medical Incubator, introducing herself to people, telling them to come watch her speak. You can't look at this kid and know that she's been on cannabis since 2013 and believe that anything bad has happened to her. Because it hasn't!"

"I THANK GOD EVERY DAY WE FOUND THIS PATH."

It was a decision no parent should ever have to make. And yet, there it was, staring Wendy Turner in the face. Her son Coltyn had been diagnosed with Crohn's disease at age 11, after nearly drowning at a Boy Scout camp and developing a bacterial infection. And, despite trying drugs like Entocort and Humera, his situation was only getting worse: His lymph nodes were swelling to the point where doctors thought he might develop T-cell lymphoma. So, by the time her son was 13, Wendy basically had three options to choose from: She could have

Coltyn, now 18, was in a wheelchair when he and father Tommy (inset) first went to Colorado.

Coltyn try another medication that might increase the chance of lymphoma. Or she could allow him to go through surgery that required removing 22 inches of diseased bowel and would leave him with a colostomy bag for the rest of his life. Then, there was a third choice: try some sort of alternative treatment outside the realm of traditional medicine.

LOOKING FOR A LIFESAVER

"He was only 13, and there was no way I was putting him through that surgery," recalls Wendy. "Our doctor said we could try alternative treatments, but he couldn't give us any information on them. That was my green light to do more research on cannabis."

As she dug into the subject, Wendy learned of an Israeli study of 21 Crohn's patients who tried medical marijuana. Eleven gained some kind of symptom relief, and nine had complete remission. There didn't seem to be any indication of detrimental side effects, so Wendy's decision was not difficult.

"Maybe Coltyn might lose some brain cells, but the treatment wasn't going to faze him," she says. "If he could be hungry and gain weight, have more energy and possibly go into remission...why *wouldn't* we try this?"

Possibly because first, the Turners lived in Illinois, which didn't have a comprehensive

> ## "
> ## OUR DOCTOR SAID WE COULD TRY ALTERNATIVE TREATMENTS, BUT HE COULDN'T GIVE US ANY INFORMATION ON THEM. THAT WAS MY GREEN LIGHT."
> **WENDY TURNER**

medical marijuana law; and second, Wendy was a typical mom who believed "pot was bad for you. We'd even kicked family members out of our lives for smoking it." But given that her son's life was at stake, she let go of the latter concern. As for the former, she solved it by sending her husband with Coltyn to Colorado, where medical marijuana became legal in 2000.

"SOMETHING WAS HAPPENING"

They found a caregiver there who started the boy off with some pot brownies and a CBD oil. And within a few days of starting with the brownies, Wendy got a call from her husband.

"He said they got cabin fever in the hotel they had to stay at since we didn't have a house there," she recalls. "They decided to take a trip up into the mountains, and when they got there, Coltyn started throwing snowballs and walking around to see the sights. A couple of weeks before that, he was in a wheelchair. Now he was running in the snow. So right then, we knew something was happening."

When Coltyn and his father returned home to Illinois, Wendy was stunned not only to see color back in his face but also to see him standing in the driveway. Within seven months of that first Colorado trip, he had gone into complete clinical remission—and the Turners were a changed family.

"It spun us around so much that we started speaking out," explains Wendy, noting that the family moved permanently to Colorado to ensure Coltyn's access to cannabis. "We thought it was important to let other kids with Crohn's know they could use this without the side effects that come with other drugs."

To get the word out about his miraculous turnaround, Coltyn started a Facebook page—Coltyn's Crue—that lobbies for more-accessible medical cannabis nationwide and features the now-18-year-old's inspirational thoughts. ("I'd rather be illegally alive than legally dead," reads one of his recent posts.) Wendy will never forget watching him watch Attorney General Jeff Sessions' confirmation hearing in early 2017.

"Coltyn lost it," she says. "Sessions said, 'My job is to uphold the law—and if you don't like the law, change it.' Coltyn heard that and said, 'We're going to Washington to change the law!' And we did go to lobby for change. We're tired of waiting."

Still, Wendy is optimistic about the future, because she's already seen it in Coltyn's smiling face.

"Every day, I think about where we'd be if we hadn't found medical cannabis," she explains. "We wouldn't have Coltyn here with us. He'd be dead. If we'd continued on the path we were on, we would have killed him—so I thank God every day we found this other path. Now we have this beautiful young man who is going to change the world."

THE FACTS ABOUT CROHN'S DISEASE

WHAT IS IT?
According to the National Institute of Diabetes and Digestive and Kidney Diseases, Crohn's is a chronic illness that inflames and irritates the digestive tract. It generally starts on a gradual basis but can worsen over time.

WHO GETS IT?
Estimates are that between 500,000 and 700,000 people in the U.S. have Crohn's disease. While it can strike at any age, it is more likely to occur in those who are between 20 and 29, those who have a family member with inflammatory bowel disease, and those who smoke. Research has found that people who have Crohn's disease in their large intestine may be more likely to develop colon cancer.

WHAT ARE THE SYMPTOMS?
Possible indications of Crohn's disease include diarrhea, stomach pain, bleeding from the rectum, fatigue, nausea, constipation and anal bleeding.

WHAT ARE THE COMPLICATIONS?
Those with Crohn's disease may experience intestinal blockage, abscesses, ulcers, anal fissures, malnutrition and inflammation in other areas of the body, such as the joints, eyes and skin.

"I'LL DO WHATEVER IS GOING TO HELP MY KIDS."

It's hard enough for a parent to deal with a tragic medical diagnosis for one of their children. So it's almost impossible to imagine what Jennifer Akridge went through after hearing in 2010 that her son Wyatt had autism and, three years later, learning that daughter Kayce had cancer. Even worse, by March 2015, 11-year-old Kayce was struggling with not only chemo but also the medications prescribed to combat its side effects, including severe headaches, pain and nausea.

Desperate for help, Akridge decided to contact CannaKids, a group she'd learned about from another parent. That's when she heard founder Tracy Ryan (p. 140) speak about the work being done not only for cancer patients but also for kids with extreme epilepsy and autism. Akridge and her husband met with pediatrician Bonni Goldstein, MD, who specializes in cannabis-oil therapy. After getting the blessing of Kayce's reluctant great-grandmother, the family started Kayce on cannabis treatments after she received the painful chemotherapy for her spine.

"My grandmother got to witness, 10 minutes after Kayce's first dose of cannabis oil, how she was able to keep something down," explains Akridge. "She was able to get up, play and laugh. After 10 minutes! That's after being bedridden. We were like, 'This is it.'"

Kayce's brother Wyatt also started on cannabis oils and began to see significant benefits as well. "He was put on three different medications—Risperdal, Vyvance, and Zoloft—at 7 years old! The Risperdal helped him sleep, but it also created aggression," says Akridge. "That's the reason I looked for [another] medication. He had gotten to the point where he

attacked an 18-month-old, and it was devastating to me."

A MARIJUANA MIRACLE

Kayce has completed chemotherapy and cannabis-oil treatment (for now), and her relieved mom says she is "thriving." Wyatt, meanwhile, stopped conventional psychological medications and is treated exclusively with cannabis oils. He has recovered enough that he can now start attending school.

Jennifer knows that despite the incredible success stories she's heard since working with CannaKids, there are still doubters who are swayed by the stigma. But as far as she is concerned, there's no arguing with the results she's observed firsthand.

"I don't care...I'll do whatever is going to help my kids," she says.

> " I CAN'T SIT BY AND LET OTHER FAMILIES SUFFER. I'M HERE FOR A PURPOSE. MY DAUGHTER'S HERE FOR A PURPOSE."
>
> **TRACY RYAN**

"HE WAS FIGHTING FOR HIS LIFE."

For Amy Dawn Bourlon-Hilterbran, the tiny town of Choctaw, Oklahoma, was more than simply her home; it was a reflection of her identity. A woman of Native American ancestry, her family had lived there for generations. "That was our place, that was our people," she explains. And then, a few years ago, she had to cut ties and leave, because she didn't want her child to die there. In 2014, Bourlon-Hilterbran's son, Austin, then 12, was on life support. His organs were failing, the result of the ever-changing pharmaceutical cocktails he'd been prescribed in order to control seizures he'd endured since he was 1 year old. "If the seizures didn't kill him first, the organ damage would likely kill him within two years," Bourlon-Hilterbran says.

Austin had been diagnosed with Dravet Syndrome, a severe form of epilepsy for which there is no cure, and the drugs seemed to be causing more damage than relief. He seized daily, and his body was shutting down. With conventional medication no longer an option, Bourlon-Hilterbran went searching for a miracle. There were none to be found in Oklahoma, where medical marijuana was illegal. She and Austin were left with no choice but to look elsewhere, specifically to cannabis-friendly Colorado, which legalized medical use in 2000 and recreational use in 2012. Her husband, Jason, Austin's stepfather (his biological dad died when he was 1), was skeptical of the benefits of cannabis and initially remained in Oklahoma with their two young sons, Nathaniel, now 7, and Freeman, now 4. Alone in an unfamiliar state, Bourlon-Hilterbran didn't know where to turn. "We had no idea if it was going to work," she says. "We didn't get any help, in any direction."

Forced to quickly educate herself, she chose a regimen of THC and THCA (the precursor chemical to THC) for Austin after learning they were the most effective treatments for kids with seizures who'd been on pharmaceuticals long-term. It took 10 months to fully wean Austin from the meds, but the first time he took THCA drops, he went three days without seizing. His mobility and speech began to improve.

"My son has never been as high on cannabis as he was on pharmaceuticals," Bourlon-Hilterbran explains. "He was a zombie who was seizing all the time. Now he's a different young man."

A LIFESAVING ROUTINE

The cannabis was working, but living apart from her family took an emotional toll on Bourlon-Hilterbran. After six months, the separation proved to be too much for Jason as well, so he left his job, packed up Nathaniel and Freeman, and joined his wife and an ever-improving Austin in Colorado.

"[Neither of us would] have believed it if we hadn't seen it ourselves," she says. "It has been amazing. Our son goes weeks or months without a seizure. He had autistic tendencies, but not any more. He just turned 16. He's happy again. He can feel one coming on; he can communicate, he knows what he needs to fix it."

These days, Austin's routine includes THC and THCA administered multiple ways— orally, via drops; on his feet, with topical creams; and through suppositories. Bourlon-Hilterbran mixes up the methods of ingestion to keep her son from building up a tolerance. "We start off with his edible in the morning. He's getting 10 milligrams of THC in the morning. He gets 100 milligrams of a four-compound specialized topical twice a day. He gets Cannatol once a day. He gets CBM once a day. Once a week, we have patches of THCA. If we hit something horrible, we'll get out the full-extract cannabis oil, much like for a cancer patient: 50 grams in 90 days." Austin's seizures haven't entirely disappeared. However, when they strike now, Cannatol intranasal spray, roll-ons and suppositories are administered. The latter have

1 / Austin (seen here with mother Amy Dawn) suffered seizures since he was 1 year old. 2 / His current medical cannabis ritual includes THC delivered orally via drops.
3 / Although her son still has some seizures, Amy Dawn says that his life is "happier and healthier" with cannabis.
4 / After Austin spent years on traditional pharmaceuticals, his mother worried they were "going to kill our kid."

apparently proven to be the most effective. They are made by Incredibles, a Colorado medical-cannabis company cofounded by Bob Eschino. The way he sees it, he's not just producing medicines. He's bringing families together. "Nothing can convince me cannabis isn't one of the most healing plants on the planet," Eschino says.

HELPING FAMILIES FIND HOPE

Now Bourlon-Hilterbran is helping those who are just beginning their journey. She cofounded the American Refugee Foundation (AMRF), which assists families who've moved to Colorado with little more than hope and a prayer. "People are coming here with terminally ill patients, and it's been too hard to find basic information. I vowed that we were going to change that," she says. AMRF now assists 300 families from 39 states and 30 countries. "We're saving lives every single day," Bourlon-Hilterbran adds.

Ultimately, she knows all too well the high price families pay to uproot in order to treat ill children and has become a fervent advocate for nationwide medical access. "We want everybody to go home," she says. "We want everybody to have access to this plant, regardless of where they live."

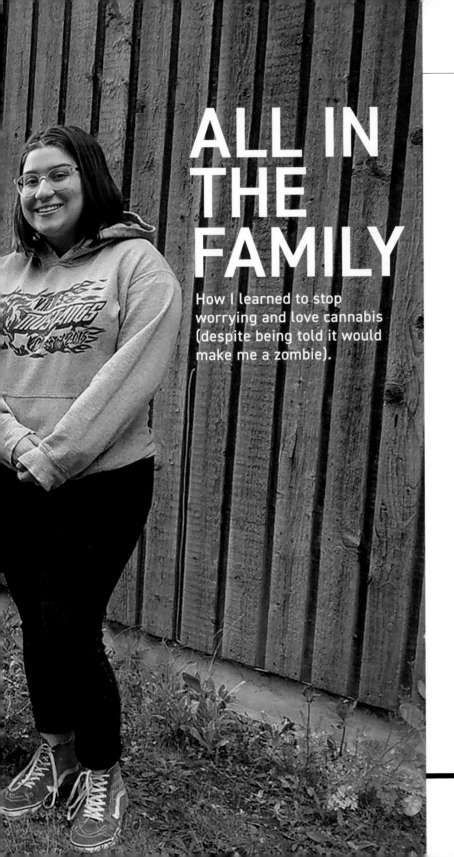

ALL IN THE FAMILY

How I learned to stop worrying and love cannabis (despite being told it would make me a zombie).

No matter how confident we like to act in public, most of us also hide some secret fear deep down inside, one that creeps up to fill us with paralyzing dread. Maybe it's the sight of a spider crawling toward you. Perhaps it's stepping onto a 50th floor balcony and then looking down. Or watching a nurse pull out a hypodermic needle to draw blood during your yearly physical.

But those all pale in comparison to the thing that inevitably makes my palms sweat and my blood pressure jump 20 points. Call it cannaphobia—fear of seeing anyone smoking marijuana. I realize that's an embarrassing thing to admit in this day and age, when one poll after another shows the popularity of pot. And yet, even as I write this sentence, I feel like I'm doing something bad just by having this discussion.

RUNNING AWAY FROM REEFER

It's a panic that's had its hooks in me since back in college, when I'd watch nervously as friends passed the bong around. As it got closer to me, I would frantically search for some excuse to get out of taking my turn. I'd say I had a cold. Or that I needed to use the bathroom. Or that I had to get up early the next morning, so no partying for me (even though I often said this while drinking a beer). I always needed to get out of any room where pot was present, because in my twisted brain, weed was something only bad people used. Inhaling it would surely turn me into an extra from the film *Reefer Madness*.

Logical? Not really. Fair? Not at all. I mean, these people were my friends. The bigger question that I never asked back then though was: Why did cannabis freak me out? Why would an educated, well-intentioned liberal thinker such as myself suddenly feel as uncomfortable as Mike Pence in the front row of a Slayer concert when marijuana was around? It's really only now, with far too many years to reflect back on, that I clearly see the source of my paranoia. It was my family.

CONTINUING CANNAPHOBIA

Sure, the relentless (and ridiculous) PSAs when I was growing up in the '70s probably influenced me. (I'm still trying to forget the one where

> ## " IN MY TWISTED BRAIN, WEED WAS SOMETHING ONLY BAD PEOPLE USED."
> **CRAIG TOMASHOFF**

some kid literally becomes a zombie after smoking a single joint, an ad made by Scooby-Doo and the Flintstones.) However, when your grandparents were solid, churchgoing Kansans and you literally never saw your parents even take a drink of alcohol, that's what truly seals the deal when it comes to your views on drug use.

I was taught to lock the car door if I saw guys with hair past their ears, because they were most certainly on drugs and might kill me for my pocket change. Ours felt to me like a solid Republican household—and if Richard Nixon blamed the ills of our nation on pot-smoking hippies, then by God, marijuana was surely the root of

all evil. Therefore, whether you used it yourself or just saw someone using it without calling the cops, rest assured you'd have plenty of time to enjoy your demon weed when you get to hell.

I've discarded plenty of other misguided lessons from my youth. The belief that eating bread crusts will make my hair curly or carrots will improve my vision, for instance. Still, the Stephen King-style treatment of marijuana kept my cannaphobia burning. Even when I finally came to terms with the truth we adults don't want our kids to know—that smoking pot is actually what cool people do—I still had a visceral reaction every time I'd see another dispensary open up in my neighborhood.

Then, reality intervened. First, I needed to find a job —any job—after three years of unemployment, and editing a marijuana magazine was my one option. And second, my back pain had become so severe that I was popping Aleves like they were Skittles. Working on the magazine introduced me to dozens of people whose lives had been changed by the medical benefits of CBD, which in turn helped me to understand that not all cannabis turns you into some drooling serial killer. Which, subsequently, meant that I had found an incredibly effective, nonaddictive way to ease my aching spine.

Infinite CBD's Freezing Point salve saved my back—and sold me on using cannabis.

TIME FOR A CHANGE

The only thing that amazed me more than my pain relief was that I decided to tell my antidrug mom about it as a way of encouraging her to try CBD for her arthritis. And...it turns out that she was already using a CBD lotion for the pain and stiffness in her neck. An idea she was willing to try, since my brother was using a CBD tincture to ease his nerve pain after back surgery. Without even realizing it, I'd suddenly become part of a cannabis-friendly family.

Now we talk about CBD as easily as we do the weather, and the change is still remarkable to me. Not so much the change in our relative medical conditions—while the new meds are great for pain management, they haven't actually cured anything—but the change in my perspective on the world in general. Seeing one of the primary sources of my fear of marijuana change her mind on the matter has shown me that the way things used to be won't dictate the way of the future. None of us is ever too old to dismiss lifelong fears and welcome new ideas.

So, with that in mind, I'm now going to eat some apple seeds without worrying a tree will grow in my stomach. And then I'll keep making that face without concern that it's going to stay like that.

—*Craig Tomashoff*

21

Food and Fun

HOME COOKING

Making a meal of marijuana is easier than you think.

The process of infusing oil with cannabis can take three hours or more.

A few years ago, when Laurie Wolf added some cannabis oil to her favorite foods, she never suspected that simple decision would place her at the forefront of a culinary revolution that only seems to get bigger by the month.

"I'm kind of shocked this is happening," says the chef and author, who is in her 60s and has been dubbed by some in the industry as "the Martha Stewart of marijuana edibles."

Wolf, who has written four cannabis-themed cookbooks, sees cooking with cannabis as being very similar to regular cooking.

There are a couple of exceptions —the food can't reach temperatures higher than 340 degrees and some of the spices have to be used in moderation. Still, the complex flavors produced by the more than 100 terpenes (the oils in cannabis that provide its aroma) in each flower lend themselves to endless gourmet possibilities, whether they're being served in an appetizer, soup, salad, entrée, dessert or cocktail. Still, she insists that the process is far easier than people might think.

"Even the beginner cook can make something delicious," Wolf says.

PEOPLE WILL
THINK
IT'S NOT
WORKING.
BUT IT IS
WORKING —
IT JUST HASN'T
HIT YOU YET.

We spoke to Wolf, and others skilled in the art of making marijuana-based meals, and they offered up these tips for those looking to cook with cannabis for the first time:

KEEP IT SIMPLE

Experts recommend starting with recipes that include olive oil, butter or coconut oil. Cannabinoids are drawn to fats and oils, which allows both the THC and CBD to become active. "This is a great starting point," says Jamie Evans, founder of The Herb Somm, a cannabis blog and lifestyle brand. "Once you infuse cannabis into butter or oil, you can add it to salad dressings, soups, hummus or pesto." Experts suggest splurging on a high-quality butter or oil.

UNDERSTAND TERPENES

"Cannabis have wonderful compounds called terpenes, which are found in different herbs, spices, flowers and essential oils," Evans says. "You'll want to find the cannabis strain that complements the meal." Some of the most common terpenes (and their flavor notes) used in cooking include pinene (pine nuts); trans-nerolido (jasmine); limonene (citrus); and caryophyllene (cloves, cinnamon).

TAKE IT SLOW

Making a weed-infused meal is no different than using cannabis in any other way: Caution is required. "When I first started, I'd add more cannabis because I'd think this is never going to work. After a couple of hours, I'd have to take a nap," Wolf says.

It also takes your body longer to process edibles. "People will think it's not working. But it is working—it just hasn't hit you yet," Evans adds. It can take between 90 minutes to two hours to feel the effects of an infused meal. Microdosing each course (consuming 1 to 5 milligrams of THC) is a good way to pace yourself while figuring out your limits.

CHOOSE YOUR MOOD

If you want to feel energized, pick a sativa (a subspecies of the cannabis plant). If you want to relax and unwind, choose an indica (another subspecies). To find the best flower for you, it's important to understand the strain's terpene profile as well as the effects of THC, CBD, THCA and other cannabinoids. For instance, if you want energy, look for strains that have a higher level of the terpene limonene. If you want to feel relaxed and sleepy, strains with higher levels of linalool are a good option.

WATCH YOUR TEMPERATURES

In order to derive the greatest potency from the cannabis plant, it's best to decarboxylate, or "decarb," the plant before infusing. Decarboxylation is the chemical reaction that releases the carboxylic acids from THC and CBD to activate the cannabis. This occurs when cannabis is exposed to heat at around 250 degrees Fahrenheit for between 30 to 60 minutes. That means keeping temperatures low to prevent the cannabis from burning. Most cooks use an oven, but you can add the raw cannabis to your slow cooker to decarb in the oil. Some cooks also rely on tools such as the MagicalButter Machine, a widely available countertop botanical extractor, which decarbs and infuses the cannabis directly into your butter, oils, tinctures and salves. To learn more about how to infuse, visit Wolf's website, laurieandmaryjane.com.

STIRRING IS KEY

Stirring the mixture well will ensure that all guests receive the same dose of THC.

DON'T BE AFRAID TO MAKE MISTAKES

Just like all recipes, cannabis cooking isn't an exact science. "The thought of having this new, infused food is exciting," Evans says. "It's definitely a science, but it's also an art. And we're all in this together, trying to figure out what works best."

HOW TO INFUSE

1 In a medium saucepan, heat the amount of oil called for in the recipe over low heat until thoroughly warmed. Add the decarbed cannabis to the oil. Stir to mix.

2 Continue to cook over low heat for 3 hours. Stir occasionally. The oil should not boil or simmer, although it may bubble occasionally.

3 Line a fine mesh strainer with cheesecloth and place it over a large, heat-safe bowl. Carefully pour the oil through the cheesecloth, allowing any excess oil to strain through. Remove the cheesecloth from the strainer, using gloves if the oil is still very hot, and squeeze any remaining oil into the bowl. Allow the oil to cool completely before transferring to an airtight container.

The key to this
mac & cheese?
A healthy helping
of cannabis butter.

MADRAS NUTS

Start to finish 25 minutes (5 active)
Servings 12

- 1 cup pecans
- 1 cup cashews
- 1 cup walnuts
- 2 tablespoons curry powder
- 1 teaspoon ground cumin
- ½ teaspoon ground cardamom
  Pinch of cayenne
  Salt to taste
  3 tablespoons canna-oil

1 Heat oven to 300°F.
2 In a large mixing bowl, combine all ingredients; mix well. Spread in single layer onto a rimmed baking sheet.
3 Bake for 20-25 minutes, stirring occasionally.
4 Allow to cool. Store in an airtight container.

Cannabis-infused oils may help illnesses such as epilepsy and cancer.

MEDICATED MAC & CHEESE

Start to finish 50 minutes (20 active)
Servings 4

- ½ pound elbow macaroni
- 1 tablespoon vegetable oil
- 1 teaspoon salt
- 4 tablespoons canna-butter
- ½ cup all-purpose flour
- 3-4 cups warm milk
- 2 cups grated sharp cheddar cheese
- 1 cup grated Gruyere cheese
- 1 cup chopped cooked broccoli
- ½ cup seeded and chopped tomatoes
- 1 teaspoon salt
- ½ teaspoon ground black pepper
- ½ teaspoon ground nutmeg
- 2 tablespoons salted butter (or canna-butter, for a stronger dose)
- 1½ cups fresh breadcrumbs
- ½ cup grated cheddar cheese

1 Heat oven to 350°F.
2 Bring a large pot of water to a boil. Add the salt and oil. Add the macaroni. Cook according to package directions. Drain well.
3 In a medium saucepan, heat the canna-butter before whisking in the flour. Cook over low heat for 5 minutes, stirring constantly with a whisk. While whisking, add the warm milk in a stream and cook for a couple of minutes, until thick and smooth. If too thick, add more milk.
4 Add the sharp cheddar, Gruyere, broccoli, tomato, salt, pepper and nutmeg. Add the cooked macaroni and stir well. Pour into 6-8 greased ramekins or a 2-quart greased casserole dish.
5 Melt remaining 2 tablespoons of butter and combine with breadcrumbs. Add remaining cheese and mix. Sprinkle on the top of the ramekins or casserole.
6 Bake for 25-30 minutes, or until the macaroni is browned on the top.

Infusing oil
or butter with
cannabis is easy
once you've tried it.

BAKED RECIPES

Try your hand at canna-cuisine
with these mouthwatering dishes.

HEMP-INFUSED GINGER CARROT SOUP

Start to finish: 50 minutes
Servings: 4

2	tablespoons Jenny's Baked Kitchen Hemp-Infused Organic Coconut Oil
1	cup diced onions
2	cups diced carrots
5	cups vegetable broth
2	full droppers Jenny's Baked Kitchen Hemp-Infused Ginger Tincture
	Salt and pepper to taste

1 In a large pot over low to medium heat (never high), sauté onions in hemp-infused coconut oil until almost translucent (about 10 to 15 minutes).
2 Add carrots and sauté until tender, 20 to 25 minutes. Stir often as the vegetables cook.
3 Add broth to pot and bring to a boil.
4 Remove pot from heat; allow to cool for several minutes.
5 Pour into blender (you may need to work in batches).
6 Add ginger tincture; blend until smooth.
7 Pour into bowls; add salt and pepper to taste.
Recipe courtesy of Jenny Argie, Baked at Home

A light soup allows you to focus on elements like which terpenes are being featured.

CBD-infused butter gives these lobster rolls a cannabis kick.

CLASSIC LOBSTER ROLLS

Start to finish: 60 minutes
Servings: 8 mini rolls

1	**3-pound live lobster**
½	**cup chopped celery**
½	**cup chopped red onion**
½	**tablespoon lemon juice**
	Salt and pepper to taste
½	**cup mayonnaise**
½	**tablespoon fresh thyme**
2	**tablespoons CBD-infused unsalted butter**
8	**mini rolls (split-top, if available)**
½	**cup microgreens**

1 In a large pot, bring water to boil. Cook lobster until bright red (about 20 minutes). Remove from pot; place lobster in an ice bath to cool.

2 Remove lobster meat from shell. Chop coarsely and place in a medium bowl.

3 Toss lobster with celery, onion, lemon juice and salt and pepper to taste. Stir in mayonnaise and thyme.

4 In small pan, melt CBD-infused butter and brush on mini rolls.

5 Toast rolls in oven until the tops are golden brown.

6 Stuff rolls with the lobster mixture and top with microgreens.

7 Serve immediately.

Recipe courtesy of Jazmine Moore, Green Panther Chef

Chef Reyes' other specialties include beef skewers and "potsicles."

IN OCTOBER 2019, THE COUNTRY'S FIRST CANNABIS CAFE OPENED IN LA. THERE'S WEED, AND THE DRINKS ARE INFUSED; THE FOOD IS NOT (YET).

INFUSED BEEF PATTIES

Start to finish 2 hours
(25 minutes active)
Servings 24 patties

- 4 cups all-purpose flour
- ½ teaspoon baking powder
- 1 teaspoon ground turmeric
- 1 teaspoon of salt
- 1 cup vegetable shortening or lard, at room temperature (look for non-hydrogenated shortening)
- 2 onions
- 3 scallions, including green tops
- 2 Scotch bonnet chilies
- 1½ pounds ground beef or chuck
- ½ cup Vireo (or other) cannabis-infused olive oil
- 1½ cups fine breadcrumbs
- ¾ teaspoon ground thyme
- ¾ teaspoon ground turmeric
  Salt and freshly ground pepper
- 1 cup water

1 In large bowl, combine flour, baking powder, turmeric and salt. Stir with whisk to blend. Cut in shortening with a pastry blender or 2 dinner knives until dough has the consistency of cornmeal.

2 Gradually add just enough cold water, mixing it in with a fork, to hold dough together. Take care not to overwork your dough; it should just come together. Form dough into a disk and wrap it in plastic wrap. Refrigerate for several hours or overnight.

3 If chilled overnight, remove the dough from the refrigerator and let sit 15 minutes before rolling out.

4 Meanwhile, make the filling: Cut up the onions, scallions and chilies. Add to the beef and mix well.

5 In a Dutch oven or large skillet, warm up Vireo oil over medium heat, then add the meat mixture and cook, stirring frequently to break up the meat, until lightly browned, about 10 minutes.

6 Stir in breadcrumbs, thyme, turmeric, salt and pepper, and water. Cover and simmer for about 20 to 30 minutes, or until thickened; the mixture should be just wet, not runny or dry. Remove from heat and let cool while you roll out the dough.

7 Preheat oven to 400°F. Divide the dough into 24 evenly sized pieces.

8 On lightly floured surface, roll out each piece of dough to a thickness of about ⅛ inch (a little thicker than pie dough). Use a drinking glass or other cutter to cut each into a circle about 4 inches across.

9 Place rounds on ungreased baking sheets about 1 inch apart. Cover the rounds you are not working on with a damp cloth.

10 Place a spoon of filling onto a round to cover half of the dough, leaving a ¼-inch border.

11 Fold the other half of the dough over the filling; use a fork to crimp the edges and seal in the filling. Repeat for remaining dough circles.

12 Bake patties for 30 to 35 minutes, or until golden. Serve hot!
Recipe courtesy of Chef Luke Reyes, La Hoja catering and events

THREE-INGREDIENT CHOCOLATE BARS

Start to finish 1 hour
(10 minutes active)
Servings 8

¼ cup pot-infused
coconut oil
3 tablespoons agave or
liquid sweetener of
choice (maple syrup
works well)
¼ organic cocoa powder
Suggested toppings:
Roasted cocoa nibs
Lemon or orange rind
Dried lavender or rose
petals
Crushed almonds
Sea salt

1 In mixing bowl, combine coconut oil and agave.
2 Add cocoa powder; stir continuously until mixture thickens. Add an extra tablespoon oil or water to thin mixture slightly, if desired.
3 Pour into confection molds (you can also spoon the mixture onto wax paper to make individual candies). Sprinkle on desired toppings.
4 Freeze or refrigerate until hardened.
Recipe courtsey of Christina Bellman, LEVO Oil

THE HOUSE THAT HEMP BUILT

What makes this Israeli house on a hill so unique? Cannabis walls, and rooms with a view.

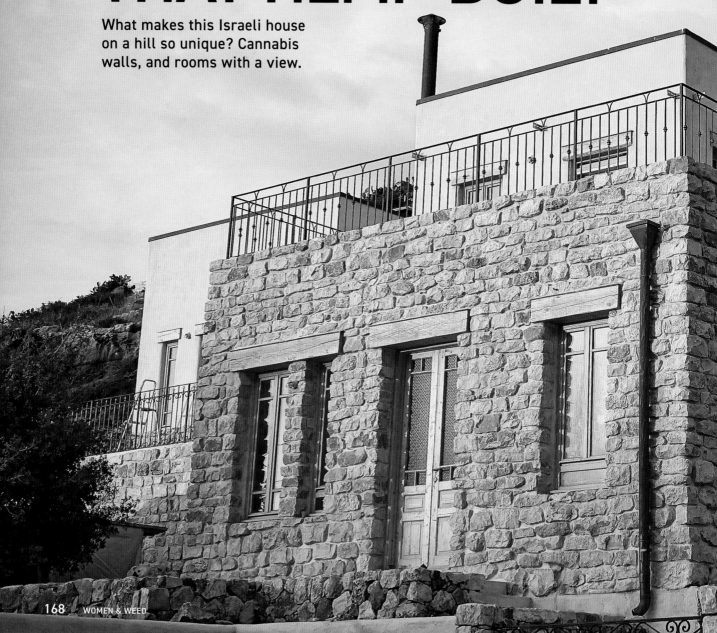

At left, the terrace of the 2,690-square-foot house faces the sea.

The Cannabis House stands on the southern slopes of the village of Ein Hod, facing the Mediterranean Sea, in northern Israel. Since its completion, the house has become an archetype of sustainability—words that architects fawn over but can make clients raise eyebrows. The evidence, however, is clear. Built in mid 2017, the house—which features a mix of hemp and lime as its core materials—has held up without fault. That should come as no surprise: Structures made of lime-based cements have been standing for hundreds of years, and early versions of hemp and lime structures have been around for more than a century.

1 / In the bathroom, a thick layer of earth-based plaster covers the hemp walls for a smooth finish. **2** / The look and feel of hemp walls remain in line with the client's wish for great design and sustainability. **3** / The kitchen is all-natural, from its design to the local products. **4** / Hempcrete walls can also be painted, as shown in this sink nook. **5** / The house blends with the beauty of its natural surroundings, using stone from the backyard.

Almost all of the materials in this home are derived from nature.

IN THE BEGINNING...

The Tav Group, pioneers of eco-architecture and design in Israel since 1987, met their perfect clients in late 2009: good friends, social activists, artists and environmental entrepreneurs. When you share a deep concern for environmental causes and are enthusiastic to build a home that advances sustainable building methods, synergy takes over.

The Tav Group suggested using hempcrete as the primary building material. The substance is created by wet-mixing the chopped woody stem (hurd) of the hemp plant with a lime-based binder to create a material that can be cast into molds, typically a timber frame, to make walls, partitions and ceilings.

Hempcrete is a natural, low-energy-consuming material that does not emit toxins during manufacture or use. It provides good thermal insulation and is porous, moderating indoor humidity. Once solidified, hempcrete becomes a limestone structural member, reinforced with hemp fiber. It's also naturally pest- and fungus-repellent and fire-resistant.

But enough usable hemp can be difficult to find. The client played an active role in searching for the right materials, traveling to France to learn firsthand about hempcrete and

ADD LOCAL STONE AND WOOD ELEMENTS AND IT PROVIDES A BEAUTIFUL SUNLIT SPACE AND A RESPITE WITH VIEWS.

then personally importing the materials.

INTERIOR DESIGN

Inside, there is a definite ease to the quiet, natural palette and simple, modern furnishings, punctuated with earth-toned rugs. Hempcrete is a very workable material, affording varying wall thicknesses, built-in niches and benches throughout the house—and architect Maoz Alon of Tav Group says, "It smells great, like freshly harvested hay in a meadow." A thick layer of earth-based plaster covers the hemp-based walls for a smooth finish. Add local stone and wooden architectural elements, and it provides a beautiful sunlit space and respite, with views of the Mediterranean Sea and breezes off the water.

The house blends with the beauty of its natural surroundings, and also includes additional workshop spaces and a private guest wing as well as solar panels, biogas production and biological toilets, to further improve its environmental footprint. The Tav Group is now adding a small roof unit using the same technology. And they are hopeful they can convince other clients to embrace this natural building material soon.

The aim: Create an archetype of sustainability, with environmentally friendly, locally sourced and natural materials, and avoid concrete altogether.

175

BETWEEN THE JOINTS

Modern-day hempcrete, a hemp-lime composite, was developed in the 1980s in France, but its roots go back centuries, from Japanese homes to Merovingian bridges.

While only around 50 homes in the United States contain hemp, there is reason to believe that domestic hemp building may be on the rise, especially if a bill that removes industrial hemp from Schedule 1 of the Controlled Substances Act and regulates it as an agricultural crop is passed.

Despite the legal red tape, hempcrete building is happening in the U.S. One of the more ambitious projects comes from an unlikely pair.

Matthew Mead is the 27-year-old founder of Hempitecture (hempitecture.com), and Pamela Bosch, 65, is a thoughtful woman who has spent most of her life in Bellingham, Washington. The duo were brought together by hemp and, in particular, hempcrete.

Bosch saw Mead's TED talk on advancing building techniques in the United States with hempcrete, and says she knew that the money she had saved for an addition to her house would go to working with him.

"It's funny," says Mead, "that she is thinking about leaving a legacy, something people can learn from, and I am thinking about the future, transforming an industry."

Benefits of Hempcrete

- Low-maintenance
- Incredible insulation
- Energy-efficient
- Flame-, water-, pest-resistant
- Lasts hundreds of years
- Strong, lightweight, breathable
- Naturally nontoxic
- Grown from seed and produced in three to four months

WANT MORE ON HEMPCRETE?

1

TheHIA.org

➜ The Hemp Industries Association is a trade association of businesses, farmers, researchers and investors working with industrial hemp.

2

OriginalGreen Distribution.com

➜ If you are looking to build with hemp, this company can match you with qualified building contractors and designers.

3

GreenBuilt.co

➜ Jim Savage promotes hempcrete through his company. He is designing a passive-energy house as a prototype for the future.

4

Hempsteads.info

➜ Builder Tim Callahan's consulting firm provides hemp building advice and resources for professionals and homeowners for projects big and small.

5

HempTech Global.com

➜ They offer building workshops for architects, builders, engineers, owners/builders, DIY enthusiasts and others.

6

AmericanLime Technology.com

➜ This company's building material, made from hemp shives (hurds) and lime-based binder products, has been used in roughly 30 projects.

Artist Taryn works exclusively with hemp fiber to create rugs and wall hangings.

ELEVATING CANNABIS DESIGN

These three companies (and entrepreneurs) are raising the bar when it comes to design, using cannabis for inspiration.

Taryn, an artist who works exclusively with hemp fibers to weave rugs and textiles, is inspired by energy, frequency and vibration—as well as the plant's sheer strength and sustainability. She experiments with shape and repetition to create patterns that suggest an infinite universal rhythm, and exhibits them through her website, Tanu.

Taryn began weaving in 2013, when she was living in an Airstream trailer and needed a new creative outlet that she could take with her on the road. "I taught myself on a small lap loom—and before long, the scale expanded beyond the confines of that lifestyle," she recalls. "So I found myself back in Denver and focused on bringing forth all the inspiration I had gathered from the road."

She began weaving with wool, but it wasn't until she started using hemp that she felt she was able to say what she wanted to on the loom. "I can stay truly aligned with the values that I created and find an authentic voice," Taryn says, referring to hemp's environmental benefits. "There is so much of the 'same same' happening all around, so having an original concept is important. We are living in a time when business has to mean more than just making money. People want to see real change happening in the world, and I believe that the most important vote we can make is the one we cast with our dollar on a daily basis. It is time to get back to a real appreciation for craft, for how our things are made, where they come from and what goes into making them."

Hemp is Taryn's Truth, and she feels that she is able to maintain a certain level of integrity so that she stays in alignment with it. "A strong vision is the first thing," she says. "If you have a vision that really inspires you, then you will have the drive and motivation to actively take the steps to bring it into the world. Discipline and time management are also key. Knowing how to effectively navigate through

Hemp bedding is soft, comfy and easy to care for.

Monica Khemsurov and Eviana Hartman, of Tetra

Taryn's bold, graphic and modern rugs are made from hemp fiber, which is 10 times stronger than cotton and can be used to make all kinds of textiles.

tasks and priorities, while still taking time to cultivate the creative energy, is essential. Top it all off with a dedicated self-care practice, whatever that looks like for you, and you're winning!" *tanuart.com*

THE ONLINE HEAD SHOP

The founders of the online Tetra shop view themselves as living in the design world. Monica Khemsurov and Eviana Hartman have spent years as design and style editors, journalists and curators. For the past three-plus years, they've also been hunting for and commissioning functional, well-designed products for smokers in a landscape that is constantly shifting. "We're not really patting ourselves on the back yet," says Hartman, "but so far, I'd say we've managed to keep going, entirely on our own terms."

Now, design enthusiasts have one place where they can access not only exclusive products from well-known designers, but also vintage accessories—including contemporary pipes, lighters, ashtrays, snuff boxes, storage containers, canisters and incense burners—that can double as décor.

A new addition is their Tetra Starter Kit: a smoked-glass ashtray, a Fog Pin (packing/cleaning tool), a Queue Stick lighter and a Tetra Balance Pipe (green or pink), all packed inside a stylish stash box.

The women consider the work of

The Tetra Shop is for enthusiasts who want accessories that double as décor.

Marianne Brandt—a German painter, sculptor, photographer and designer who studied at the Bauhaus school—a timeless example of modern industrial design, and an inspiration. They also hold up Katja Blichfeld, the cocreator of the HBO comedy *High Maintenance*, which follows a nameless weed deliveryman through New York. They have a simple business philosophy: Start small and focused. Don't try to be everything all at once. Know your strengths and try to set up something that will allow you to do what you're good at and what you uniquely offer. Sell something that people will continuously buy. And a single vision of an ideal day? A long afternoon on the beach or in the woods, with loved ones—and without a smartphone. *shop-tetra.com*

HEMP AT HOME

Rob Jungmann has been working with hemp since 1993, but the plant really took hold of him years before. "As a kid, on trips to the Washington State mountains, I would camp out in the woods with beautiful trees. Each year, when we returned, I noticed a clear cut…more every year." Fast-forward to college and an environmental studies course where the professor mentioned industrial hemp as an alternative crop to prevent devastation of landscapes. The dots started to connect, and an idea formed.

After graduation, Jungmann began to make things. What started as one company that designed twill-fabric shoirts and shorts, messenger bags and mountaineering chalk bags to accommodate his youthful lifestyle of biking and mountain climbing, ended with another company, Jungmaven, that focused on a single item, the T-shirt. Both had one thing in common: hemp.

Jungmaven's marketing goal is to have everyone in a hemp tee by 2020. "But what I really mean is, get everyone talking about it," says Jungmann. He focused on getting the texture, color, feel and even the label perfect, working with imported textiles (domestic hemp is still lurking in a gray area in the U.S.) and finishing off the design stateside.

Then came the call. "One of my suppliers asked if we wanted to try hemp bedding," recalls Jungmann. "I slept on it the first night and was transported. I had an incredible sleep." Like linen, the hemp weave gets softer with each wash, but stays textured. What's most luxurious about the hemp weave is its heavy weight and breathability (it allows air to pass through it easily, so it doesn't become warm or uncomfortable). Fabric care is the same as for most materials—100 percent hemp, naturally washed and unbleached, can easily be machine-washed and tumble-dried.

Also in the works are hand-dyed indigo hemp sheets. While the design is custom-only at the moment, the company hopes to see it as an in-stock item in the future. *jungmaven.com*

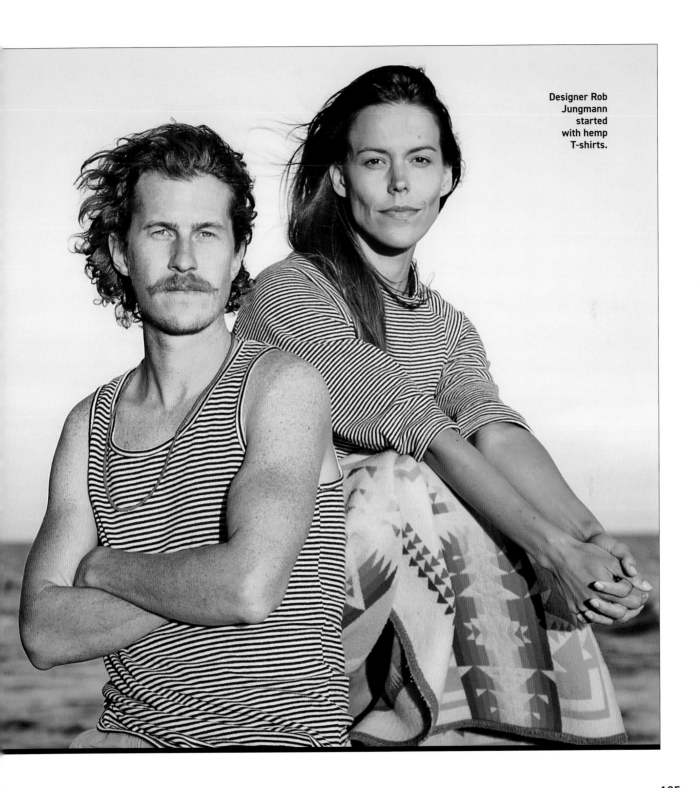

Designer Rob Jungmann started with hemp T-shirts.

Cover DigitalVision Vectors/Getty Images **2-3** Maya Karkalicheva/Getty Images **4-5** E+/Getty Images **7** Alamy **8** Yuttana Jindaluang/Alamy **9** Shutterstock/golddiamondphotography; Shutterstock/Taylor Wilson **10** Jeff Rotman/Getty Images; Moment/Getty Images **11** MediaNews Group/Getty Images; Heath Korvola/Getty Images **12** Shutterstock/Fascinadora; Kivilcim Pinar/Getty Images; iStockphoto **13** Shutterstock/Misha Beliy **14-15** Cameron Zegers/Stocksy **16-17** Getty Images **18** Corbis/Getty Images **19** Getty Images/iStockphoto **20** Getty Images; OJO Images/Getty Images; Corbis/Getty Images; Getty Images/iStockphoto; Alamy; Shutterstock/Brandon Crawford **21** Alamy; Corbis/Getty Images **22** Getty Images/Ikon Images **24** Shutterstock/kostrez **25** Shutterstock/ElRoi **26** Shutterstock/Doug Shutterstock **27** Shutterstock/ElRoi **28-29** Shutterstock/Alexander_Volkov **30-31** bortonia/Getty Images **32** Getty Images **33** bortonia/Getty Images **34-35** Digital Vision/Getty Images **38** AFP/Getty Images **40** PA Images/Getty Images **41** Alamy **42** igorbondarenko/Getty Images **43** Getty Images/EyeEm Premium **44** Getty Images/iStockphoto **45** Alamy; Popperfoto/Getty Images **46** Hulton Archive/Getty Images **47** Getty Images **48** LIFE Images/Getty Images; Associated Press **49** CQ-Roll Call/Getty Images; Getty Images/Science Photo Library **51** Getty Images/fStop **53** Corbis/Getty Images **55** Getty Images/Westend61 **57** E+/Getty Images **58-59** Shutterstock/Vanessa Bentley **60-61** Jade Brookbank/Getty Images **63** Tetra images/Getty Images **65** Hero Images/Getty Images **66-67** Alamy Stock Photo **68** Kristina Strasunske/Getty Images **70-71** Getty Images/iStockphoto; Sodatech AG, Switzerland/Stock Pot Images (2); Maren Caruso/Getty Images; Sodatech AG, Switzerland/Stock Pot Images; Maren Caruso/Getty Images **72-73** Getty Images/iStockphoto; Sodatech AG, Switzerland/Stock Pot Images (3) Maren Caruso/Getty Images **74-75** Getty Images/iStockphoto; Sodatech AG, Switzerland/Stock Pot Images (3) **76** E+/Getty Images **80-81** Denver Post via Getty Images **82-83** Heath Korvola/Getty Images **85** E+/Getty Images **87** Klaus Vedfelt/Getty Images **89** Klaus Vedfelt/Getty Images **90-91** E+/Getty Images **93** Digital Vision/Getty Images **94-95** Jeff Chiu/AP Photo **96** Getty Images **98** Getty Images/Blend Images **100** E+/Getty Images; Shutterstock/Gelner Tivadar; NurPhoto via Getty Images; James Baigrie/Getty Images **103** Getty Images **104-105** Getty Images/Tetra images RF **108-109** Kristen Angelo **110** Alamy **112-113** Shutterstock/Roxana Gonzalez **115** Heath Korvola/Getty Images **117** Gail Johnson/Getty Images **118-119** E+/Getty Images **121** Getty Images/Hero Images **122** E+/Getty Images **124-125** Getty Images **126** E+/Getty Images **128** Taxi/Getty Images **131** Taxi/Getty Images **132** Manufoto **134-135** iStock/Getty Images **136-137** Robyn Beck/Getty Images **139** Shutterstock/Roxana Gonzalez **140-141** Leah Moriyama **142-143** Jen Castle **150-151** Craig Tomaschoff **155** Lew Robertson/Getty Images **156** offset/Shutterstock **157** iStock/Getty Images **158-159** Bruce Wolf **160-161** Bruce Wolf; Shutterstock/New Africa **162-163** Istetiana/Getty Images **164-165** Getty Images/iStockphoto, The Green Panther Chef **166** istetiana/Getty Images **168-169** Tavgroup **170-175** Yaeli Gabrieli (7)

DISCLAIMER Laws regarding marijuana use and regulation vary by jurisdiction and are subject to change. Please consult with a professional before using cannabis for medical treatment.

SPECIAL THANKS TO CONTRIBUTING WRITERS

Shira Adler, Lynne Blum, Kate Botta, Barbara Brody, Joanne Cachapero,
Tom Cunneff, Kerstin Czarra, Anne Driscoll, Erik Himmelsbach-Weinstein,
Scottie Jeanette Madden, Peter Rugg, Craig Tomashoff

CENTENNIAL BOOKS

An Imprint of
Centennial Media, LLC
40 Worth St., 10th Floor
New York, NY 10013, U.S.A.

CENTENNIAL BOOKS is a trademark of Centennial Media, LLC

ISBN 978-1-951274-09-2

Distributed by
Simon & Schuster, Inc.
1230 Avenue of the Americas
New York, NY 10020, U.S.A.

For information about custom editions, special sales and premium and corporate purchases,
please contact Centennial Media at contact@centennialmedia.com.

Manufactured in China

Publishers & Co-Founders Ben Harris, Sebastian Raatz
Editorial Director Annabel Vered
Creative Director Jessica Power
Executive Editor Janet Giovanelli
Deputy Editor Alyssa Shaffer
Design Director Ben Margherita
Senior Art Director Laurene Chavez
Art Directors Natali Suasnavas, Joseph Ulatowski
Production Manager Paul Rodina
Production Assistant Alyssa Swiderski
Editorial Assistant Tiana Schippa
Sales & Marketing Jeremy Nurnberg